Unshakeable Peace

The Life and Times
of Haggai the Prophet

by Kelley Varner

Destiny Image Publishers
P.O. Box 310
Shippensburg, PA 17257
"Speaking to the Purposes of God for this Generation
and for the Generations to Come"
ISBN 1-56043-137-7
For Worldwide Distribution
Printed in the U.S.A.

Destiny Image books are available through these fine distributors outside the United States:

Christian Growth, Inc.
Jalan Kilang-Timor, Singapore 0315

Lifestream
Nottingham, England

Rhema Ministries Trading
Randburg, South Africa

Salvation Book Centre
Petaling, Jaya, Malaysia

Successful Christian Living
Capetown, Rep. of South Africa

Vision Resources
Ponsonby, Auckland, New Zealand

WA Buchanan Company
Geebung, Queensland, Australia

Word Alive
Niverville, Manitoba, Canada

Inside the U.S., call toll free to order:
1-800-722-6774

Acknowledgments

To all the local churches and individuals, whose gifts made this project possible.

To pastor Gary Rich, for the initial inspiration to write this book.

To psalmist John Houston, for the song of the Lord about unshakeable peace.

To the Holy Spirit, who is my Teacher.

Dedication

Mt. 5:9, NIV

Blessed are the peacemakers, for they will be called sons of God.

Haggai was the Lord's messenger in the Lord's message (Hag. 1:13). Such men are rare. Mature sons, like real apostles, are hard to find. I wanted to dedicate this book to someone in whom I have witnessed unshakeable peace, to give honor to whom honor is due.

One word describes this father to the Body of Christ: He is *gracious*. This individual is a crafty veteran of the good fight of faith, and like Paul, has the battle scars to prove it. Some men preach about sonship—this brother has lived it. In the Kingdom of God his voice is distinguished with an ability to communicate clearly the deep things of the Spirit whether the audience be comprised of his grandchildren or a room full of preachers. Most noticeably, this seasoned minister is an ambassador of peace. Apostle, pastor, theologian, author, father to many—I am honored that this man is my friend and brother.

To Mel Bailey and his lovely companion Rhonda, you have blessed and inspired my life.

About the Cover

God has blessed us with the ability to perceive words in the form of pictures. These pictures are filtered through our life experiences to reveal an image that is unique to each of us. No one else will *see* an image the way you do. When we see or hear the words *unshakeable peace*, the image that you see is different from the image I see. I see a majestic mountain carved into a tablet of marble. You may see a stream or a meadow, depending on the situations and events you have experienced.

Spiritual perception operates differently. Instead of seeing different images, we begin to see a common image. It is an image of God's peace filtered through the experience of His death and resurrection. It reveals a perfect picture of who He is and what we will become. This picture of peace is much different than the other picture, however; this picture transforms us into that which we see, when we see Him we will be like Him, because we shall see Him as He is.

Tony Laidig
Artist

Table of Contents

Part Four
The Prince of Unshakeable Peace—
The Whole Dominion!

Foreword

The Book of Haggai has great prophetic significance for our generation. Its message is for those who have the integrity to honestly acknowledge present conditions without losing sight of the fact that God's purpose is still very much alive. The Church, as in the days of Haggai, needs a prophetic stirring from God. We must be reconnected to the only thing God is really doing in the earth—building a habitation for Himself.

We live in a time of growing hunger, a time when many searching hearts feel lost, dissatisfied with, and unrelated to much that is being offered in the name of God's work. Many have given themselves to unworthy and inferior purposes. Now they feel all used up with very little left to contribute.

This writing will be a source of encouragement to many weary ministries. The message of Haggai is very confronting, yet it offers much hope for our present state. We must acknowledge that we live in a time of great spiritual drought, failure, and famine. Very little that we do is being promoted as the ultimate fullness of what God wants to do.

This book will adjust our motives and vision of what we are willing to settle for as God's real work. The end result will be the raising up of a house of greater glory and unshakeable peace, able to withstand a period of great global shaking.

The days ahead will make us thankful for our brother Kelley Varner and his desire to put this message into print. Thank you, Kelley, for your obedience.

Pastor Gary Rich
New Foundation Church
Easley, South Carolina

Preface

The Body of Christ is a disjointed army. It is an incomplete temple in urgent need of much repair and reconstruction; it is little more than disconnected bones and burnt stones. Men busy themselves with private agendas and substitute goals while ignoring the reality of their true spiritual condition. For many, the day of revival and restoration seems to be over. Still hurting from past relationships, the thought of reconnecting to the Lord's work, the original vision, is most disturbing to them.

My last book, *Rest in the Day of Trouble*, chronicled the life and times of Habakkuk, the prophet who proclaimed God's word just prior to Jerusalem's invasion and subsequent captivity in Babylon. Haggai, the first post-exilic visionary to the returning remnant, prophesied about 100 years later.

There are many voices in the world, each with its distinctive beckon. These serious days demand wise choices. As in Haggai's time, God has sent a drought to His people. We have looked for much, but it has come to little. We must have real answers. What is the word of the Lord? Who is really speaking it? Jesus is cleansing His temple in the day of overturning. The Church that He builds, the latter house of greater glory, will be marked by an *unshakeable peace* in the time of global shaking!

Haggai's message progressively unfolds the revelation of His never-failing peace, showing forth its purpose, parameter, purity, and Prince—the Lord Jesus Christ. His finished work provided redemption for the whole man, and His glory stands poised to fill the whole earth. His corporate house is stepping forward to offer Him its whole heart in pure worship, to give Him the whole dominion, to proclaim Him Lord of all!

Pastor Kelley Varner
Praise Tabernacle
Richlands, North Carolina

This message was delivered at a recent conference at Niagra Ministries, New York, where Joanne Bunce served as host pastor. As the Word was preached, John Houston, a prophetic psalmist from North Carolina, was given this song of the Lord. He graciously granted me permission to share it with you.

Unshakeable Peace

I will be glorified in My holy temple,
My house shall be filled with a sweet holy sound,
Then I shall restore all the years that were stolen,
Establish My life in you...you shall be holy ground.

I will be glorified. This is just the beginning,
The unveiling of truth, complete and fulfilled.
I will pour out the oil, the new wine will flow freely;
You shall walk in My power, becoming My will.

I will be glorified. You will be My sweet fragrance,
All the winds of the earth shall then carry abroad
This aroma of holiness to all lands and all nations,
They shall see in My people; truly I am your God.

I will be glorified; in your midst I will prosper,
When the earth groans with fear, you shall be My release.
I will prove My great power and will give you this hour,
In the time of great shaking, My unshakeable peace....

John Houston
March 19, 1994

Chapter One

Introduction

Haggai was Heaven's first prophetic voice to the Jewish remnant following the Babylonian captivity. He, his contemporary Zechariah, and then Malachi (who ministered in the days of Nehemiah) are the three post-exilic prophets of the restoration period who finalize the Old Testament canon.

To fully appreciate this brief and oft-neglected Old Testament book, one must know about the prophet himself, appreciate the difficult days in which he ministered, and examine the swift, singular message that he proclaimed. So let us take a fresh look at Haggai—the man, the moment, the message.

The Man

Ezra 5:1-2, NIV

Now Haggai the prophet and Zechariah the prophet, a descendant of Iddo, prophesied to the Jews in Judah and Jerusalem in the name of the God of Israel, who was over them.

Then Zerubbabel son of Shealtiel and Jeshua son of Jozadak set to work to rebuild the house of God in Jerusalem. And the prophets of God were with them, helping them.

Ezra 6:14, NIV

So the elders of the Jews continued to build and prosper under the preaching of Haggai the prophet and Zechariah, a descendant of Iddo. They finished building the temple according to the command of the God of Israel and the decrees of Cyrus, Darius and Artaxerxes, kings of Persia.

Like Noah and John the Baptist, Haggai—the prophet of reconstruction—was a no-holds-barred preacher of repentance. Very little is known about this man who preached in the sixth, seventh, and ninth months of 520 B.C. Zechariah brought a confirming word in the eighth and eleventh months of that same year (Zech. 1:1,7). Their names are associated in the Septuagint (LXX) with the titles of Psalms 137 and 145-148, and in the Latin Vulgate with Psalms 111 and 145. Haggai challenged the people to build Zerubbabel's temple. Zechariah encouraged them to behold the spiritual temple, the Messiah's Church. Haggai was practical, with his feet on the ground. Zechariah was visionary, with his head in the clouds—they were a great combination.

Nothing is known about Haggai's life, before or after his public ministry. His place in time is marked by the word he prophesied! Haggai is called "the prophet" five times and "the Lord's messenger" once (Hag. 1:13). No seer ever appeared at a more critical juncture in Jewish history, nor was any more successful. Nothing is known about his family or social circumstance, not even his father's name. Jerome's commentary suggests a Levitical descent; tradition buried him with honor near the sepulchres of the priests.

"Haggai" is the Hebrew word *Chagay*. (See #2292 in James Strong's *The Exhaustive Concordance of the Bible* [Peabody, MA: Hendrickson Publishers, n.d.]). It means "festive." This word comes from *chag* (Strong's #2282) meaning "a festival, or a victim therefore"; its root *chagag* (Strong's #2287) means "to move in a circle, to march in a sacred procession, to observe a festival; by implication, to be giddy." The latter is translated in the King James Version as "celebrate, dance, keep or hold a (solemn) feast (holy day), reel to and fro." His name appears in the Septuagint (LXX) as *Aggaios* and in the Latin Vulgate as *Aggaeus*. Compare Genesis 46:16, Numbers 26:15, Second Samuel 3:4, and First Chronicles 6:30.

Thus, "Haggai" means "the joyous one, festal one, rejoicing; feast of Jehovah, my feast, festival." The foundations of Zerubbabel's temple were laid amidst shouts and tears of joy (Ezra 3:12; 5:16); it was God's desire that the remnant continue, and complete their labors in a festive spirit. The etymology of Haggai's moniker highlights and anticipates the glorious Church as the joy of the whole earth in the Feast of Tabernacles, a major theme of his prophecy (Ps. 48:1-2).

Some suggest Haggai to have been an old man, one of those who remembered Solomon's Temple (Hag. 2:3). But he and Zechariah were probably young men who

their parents from Babylon as chil-
prophets would have witnessed the morale of
the remnant steadily deteriorating, then received their
commissions from God to speak out.

Haggai exhorted the returning Jews to revive their
work on finishing the second temple. The bulk of his
prophecy is personal, addressed to the governor Zerubbabel and the high priest Joshua. The remainder of his
oracle contains rebuke and encouragement for the
priests and people. Interwoven among his declarations
concerning Zerubbabel's temple are predictions pertain-
ing to the real spiritual temple, the New Testament
revelation of Jesus Christ and His glorious Church.

Haggai—The Moment

Haggai's ministry took place under Darius I (Hystaspis), king over Persia from 521-486 B.C. The historical
background for Haggai's prophecy is narrated in the first
six chapters of the Book of Ezra.

In 536 B.C. Zerubbabel (the governor of Judah) and
Joshua (or Jeshua) the priest returned to Jerusalem with almost 50,000 exiles (Ezra 1-2). Permission to rebuild the
temple had been granted by King Cyrus (538 B.C.), the conqueror of Babylon. With great joy the altar of burnt offerings had been reconstructed, some Levitical public
worship was restored, and the foundation of the second
temple had been laid (Ezra 3). Chapter four of Ezra recounts
how the Samaritan opposition discouraged and stopped the
enterprise. Fifteen years passed with no further work on the
House of God. Finally, in the autumn of 520 B.C., Haggai
and Zechariah brought forth their admonition to finish the

task (Ezra 5). Consequently, the temple was completed and dedicated (Ezra 6).

Two major figures are addressed in Haggai's prophecy—Zerubbabel and Joshua, who respectively reveal the principles of king and priest (Zech. 6:13). Zerubbabel is called Sheshbazzar in the Book of Ezra (Ezra 1:8; 5:14,16). The grandson of Jehoiachin (1 Chron. 3:17-19), he was appointed by Cyrus to be governor of Judah. Joshua (called Jeshua in the Book of Ezra) was the son of Jehozadak, the high priest at the time of Babylon's invasion (1 Chron. 6:15).

The first person mentioned in the Book of Ezra is Cyrus, king of Persia. Isaiah, who ministered from 745-695 B.C., had pinpointed the coming of this monarch over 150 years before his birth (Is. 44:28; 45:13). He summoned Cyrus by name and predicted that he would rebuild the temple, which in the prophet Isaiah's day had not yet fallen! The Jewish historian Josephus contends that Isaiah's scroll was discovered by the Persian king, noting that "when Cyrus read this, and admired the Divine power, an earnest desire and ambition seized upon him to fulfill what was so written…" (Ant. XI. 1.2 in *The Complete Works of Flavius Josephus* [Grand Rapids, MI: Kregel Publications, 1960]).

"Cyrus" means "the sun, rays of the sun; perhaps, a shepherd." Besides Isaiah and the Book of Ezra, Cyrus is mentioned a total of 22 times in the Bible (see 2 Chron. 36:22-23; Dan. 1:21; 6:28; 10:1). In 539 B.C., after Cyrus conquered Nabonidus, king of Babylon, he presented himself as a gracious liberator and benefactor to the priests and people. A notable feature of the Persian empire was its integration of diverse peoples into a single administrative system while maintaining a respect for their local customs and beliefs. The so-called Cyrus Cylinder gives his own account of this:

> ...I returned to sacred cities on the other side of the Tigris, the sanctuaries of which have been ruins for a long time...and established for them permanent sanctuaries. I also gathered all their former inhabitants and returned to them their habitations (*The Zondervan Pictorial Encyclopedia of the Bible,* Vol. 1 [Grand Rapids, MI: Zondervan Publishing House, 1975] p. 1056).

In the restoration books of Ezra, Nehemiah, and Esther, as well as in the prophetic writings of Ezekiel and Daniel, these sovereign decrees point to the authority of the Lord Jesus Christ, our New Testament "King of kings" (see Ezra 7:12; Ezek. 26:7; Dan. 2:37; 1 Tim. 6:15; Rev. 17:14). King Cyrus thus prefigures the Lord Jesus; his grand edict to release and restore the Jews foreshadows the Great Commission (Mt. 28:18-20; Mk. 16:15-20; Acts 1:8). Cyrus' proclamation pictures the sovereign decree of the heavenlies—"the volume of the book" concerning Jesus and His Church (Heb. 10:7).

Jeremiah had prophesied that Judah would serve Babylon for 70 years (Jer. 25:10-11; Dan. 9:1-2; Zech. 1:12). He declared a dual fulfillment: a time of captivity and a time of desolations. The first deportees were carried into the strange land in 606 B.C. Seventy years later, the captives returned to Jerusalem. The temple was destroyed in 586 B.C. Seventy years later, it was rebuilt and dedicated.

Most of the exiled Jews had settled in Babylon, built houses and businesses, planted gardens, married, and raised families. By 536 B.C., those born in captivity were more than 50 years old, with children and grandchildren of their own. Not all wanted to tear up established roots and return to a unknown land. A sizable community remained in Babylon for centuries, becoming a center of Jewish scholarship that eventually produced the Babylonian Talmud. Most of God's people were more interested in temporal prosperity than their spiritual destination. Only a fraction of the refugees made the first trip with Zerubbabel, including only four of the 24 orders of priests; five out of six "preachers" stayed in Babylon (Ezra 2:36-39). There were two other subsequent returns—one under Ezra 80 years later (458 B.C.), then another with Nehemiah (445 B.C.).

By 520 B.C., the reconstruction site had been sitting empty for 15 years. The Samaritan uprising, a lukewarm remnant, and the decree of Artaxerxes (Cyrus' successor) had halted all building operations. The people had become complacent, enraptured with their own well-being, abandoning the game plan to a future generation. Isaiah had forecast their deliverance in terms that were reminiscent of the Exodus. But there had been no cruel bondage in Babylon. Zerubbabel was no Moses. Joshua Ben-Jehozadak was not Joshua son of Nun empowered to dispossess giants and walled cities.

Under Assyrian and Babylonian policies concerning displaced persons, those least capable of revolt had been left in the land, and conquered foreigners had been brought in. Jerusalem was destroyed, not rebuilt; the land was ravaged, not reclaimed. When Assyria over-powered the northern kingdom Israel (722 B.C.) and Babylon carried away Judah (586 B.C.), the conquerors had left a mixed multitude in the land. These mongrel idol worshipers did not fear the Lord (2 Kings 17:32-33). Men always want covenant with God on their own terms, His blessing without His divine procedure. The Samaritans were marked by the identity of many strange religions. Zerubbabel and Joshua refused the unequal yoke with these idol worshipers and reaped much per-secution. These worldly people had frustrated and even-tually outlawed the work of the Lord. A strong prophetic voice was needed to stir the remnant back to the original vision of building God's house.

Haggai—The Message

Enter Haggai, a man on a mission, a heavenly ambas-sador with but one message, one idea. The prophet rep-resented *Jehovah-Tsebaoth*, "the Lord of hosts," the Source of all power, the Controller of armies on earth and in Heaven. The Lord of hosts had authority—the weather obeyed His commands (Hag. 1:11); the whole universe was in His grasp and would one day be shaken by His mighty hand (Hag. 2:6,21).

The contents of Haggai's prophecy are worth examin-ing. Haggai himself is mentioned nine times. This powerful man boldly declared His divine commission. The key expression mentioned five times in the King James Version is "the Word of the Lord." In the 38 verses of Haggai's oracle, "Jah of hosts" is cited 14 times and

"Jah," 19 times. The key words to the Book of Haggai are "day" (11 times), "house (of the Lord)" (8 times), and "consider" (5 times). The key verse, Haggai 1:8, sets forth the original commission to "...build the House...." Haggai's primary message is that the temple, the house of the Lord, must be consummated and crowned with divine glory and peace! Other related thoughts and practical lessons from his prophecy are:

1. *We have received an apostolic call to a work of faith in the face of adversity (1 Cor. 15:58).*

2. *The cure for discouragement is "the Word of the Lord."*

3. *Holiness is not contagious, but sin is.*

4. *Life's problems lie not with the times and conditions of the day, but with the hearts of the people.*

5. *A lack of prosperity is the result of neglecting the house of the Lord.*

6. *God and His house must be first in the life and service of the redeemed (Mt. 6:33).*

7. *Do not become weary in well doing (Gal. 6:9).*

8. *God's promise for tomorrow is our hope for today.*

9. *National adversity is generally due to national disobedience to God.*

10. *Resignation is a killer of faith.*

The Book of Haggai is naturally divided by his four addresses. The internal evidence of the text formats and outlines itself:

1. *The call to build, to arouse.*

Haggai's opening address (Hag. 1:1-15) was a word of reproof and rebuke to Zerubbabel, Joshua, and the people about the temple's construction. It came on the first day of Elul (August-September). This first prophecy exhorts the remnant to finish the sanctuary. Zerubbabel was from David's house, Joshua from Aaron's (1:1)—God had preserved the Messianic seed through the years of captivity. The people, more interested in their own private lives, made excuse that the time to rebuild had not yet come (1:2,4). Consequently, their labor had lacked Jehovah's blessing (1:5-6). They had failed to pay heed to the Word of the Lord; now they reaped the consequences. The Jews then honored the Lord by obeying Haggai's admonition, and they resumed the work (1:8,12). God acknowledged their response with the assurance of His presence and rescued His people from fear and indifference (1:13-14). The remnant resumed the work just 23 days after Haggai began to prophesy (1:15).

2. *The call to courage, to support.*

Haggai's second address (Hag. 2:1-9) was a word of encouragement to Zerubbabel and Joshua about the temple's completion. It came on the twenty-first day of Tishri (September-October). This second utterance was directed to the aged refugees (2:3). Haggai encouraged the remnant in their distress over Zerubbabel's project, for they were without means to equal the former house (2:4-5). He predicts that the New Testament temple would exceed Solomon's in magnificence; the silver and gold belonged to Jehovah (2:7-9). He upset Egypt in the days of Passover; He would yet shake the heavens and the earth (2:5-7). The Desire of all nations would come forth in the day when the latter house was filled with His glory and peace (Hag. 2:7-9).

3. The call to separation, to confirm.

Haggai's third address (Hag. 2:10-19) was a word of correction to the priests about the temple's worship. It came on the twenty-fourth day of Chisleu (November-December). This third discourse was to the priests and the people. The faint aroma of sanctity coming from their altar's sacrifices was too feeble to pervade the secular atmosphere of their daily lives. The temple's ruined skeleton lay like a dead body decaying in Jerusalem, contaminating everything. The priests replied that whatever touched the hallowed flesh did not become holy, but a polluted person contaminated everything he touched (2:12-13). Working on the sanctuary would not make them holy; rather, their attitudes had desecrated God's house and spoiled their efforts (2:14). The people had failed to respond to Jehovah's disciplinary judgment (2:17). However, the blessing of obedience extends to material things, and would be made possible by a new beginning in God (2:19).

4. The call to faith for the future, to assure.

Haggai's final address (Hag. 2:20-23) was the special word of promise to Zerubbabel about the temple's strength and the Messiah's authority. It came on the twenty-fourth day of Chisleu (November-December). Haggai's final oracle, a personal message to Zerubbabel, predicted the overthrow of Gentile powers (2:21-22).

governor of Judah, would become God's signature-ring of total authority and government (2:23).

The central, foundational theme of Haggai's prophecy has to do with *unshakeable peace*—unbreakable relationships, unbroken covenants, undivided hearts. His prophetic paradigm unfolds as:

1. *The Purpose of Unshakeable Peace—The Whole Man!*

   a. *1:1-4—The Rebuke.*
   b. *1:5-11—The Remedy.*
   c. *1:12-15—The Resolve.*

2. *The Parameter of Unshakeable Peace—The Whole Earth!*

   a. *2:1-5—The Remembrance.*
   b. *2:6-9—The Release.*

3. *The Purity of Unshakeable Peace—The Whole Heart!*

   a. *2:10-14—The Repair.*
   b. *2:15-19—The Reward.*

4. *The Prince of Unshakeable Peace—The Whole Dominion!*

   a. *2:20-22—The Removal.*
   b. *2:23—The Ruler.*

Haggai, the book of restoration, could also be outlined as:

1. *The Call to Correction (1:1-15).*

2. *The Call to Courage (2:1-9).*

3. *The Call to Cleansing (2:10-19).*

4. *The Call to Confidence (2:20-23).*

Or:

1. *The Ruin (1:1-11).*

2. *The Rebuilding (1:12-15).*

3. *The Restoration (2:1-9).*

4. *The Reflection (2:10-19).*

5. *The Rest (2:20-23).*

The Book of Haggai is Messianic. Jesus Christ is revealed as Prophet (Haggai), Priest (Joshua), and Prince or King (Zerubbabel), uniting the three offices in one Person. The Lord Jesus Christ, the One with all power:

1. *Is the Builder of the Father's house, the Church (Mt. 16:18; Heb. 3:5-6).*

2. *Is the Restorer of the temple's glory (Hag. 2:7-9; Heb. 1:1-4).*

3. *Is the Foundation and the Altar of the real temple (Hag. 2:18; 1 Cor. 3:11; Heb. 13:10).*

4. *Is the Overthrower of all worldly kingdoms (Hag. 2:22; Rev. 11:15).*

5. *Is the Signet Ring (Hag. 2:23; Mt. 28:18).*

Most of all, King Jesus is the Source of unwavering peace (Eph. 2:14)! Haggai speaks to our generation concerning the restoration of God's house and the glorious One who lives there. Zion, the Kingdom of God, will never be moved (Ps. 125:1-2). It is the habitation of God, the place of unshakeable peace and unbroken covenant.

Come now to a time over 500 years before Messiah's birth. The voice of a young prophet is about to pierce the ironclad allegiance of a people determined to preserve their lukewarm life style. The living Word is postured and focused to revive the original vision of the God of Abraham and David.

Part One

The Purpose Of Unshakeable Peace— The Whole Man!

Chapter Two

The Rebuke

"Is it time...?"

Haggai 1:1-4

Harvesttime had arrived, September, 520 B.C. A century had passed since Habakkuk and Jeremiah predicted the Chaldean invasion and an exile that would last 70 years (Jer. 25:8-11). Their term of confinement was ended; a righteous remnant had followed Zerubbabel back to the land of their fathers. The brazen altar had been set back on its base and the foundation of the second temple was laid. The Samaritan protest had caused their endeavor to cease from force and power it aroused against them (Ezra 4:23). Now, almost 15 years later, the house of God still lay in ruin and rubble. Neglect and lethargy ruled the city. Suddenly, a fresh, young voice cut through the selfish unbelief of a tired remnant, "Consider your ways!"

This People

Hag. 1:1-2, KJV

*In the second year of Darius the king, in the sixth
month, in the first day of the month, came the word of
the Lord by Haggai the prophet unto Zerubbabel the son
of Shealtiel, governor of Judah, and to Joshua the son of
Josedech, the high priest, saying,*

*Thus speaketh the Lord of hosts, saying, This people
say, The time is not come, the time that the Lord's house
should be built.*

This Darius (his title) was Hystaspis, "king" of Persia,
who reigned from 521-468 B.C. (Ezra 4:24-6:22); his
"second year" was 520 B.C. "Darius" means "one who con-
serves; one who restrains; upholding the good." Haggai
sounded his trumpet on "the first day of the month," the
new moon in the lunar calendar (Ps. 81:3), the perfect oc-
casion to gain the ear of his farming community. On such
a day, the lack of a house of worship would be felt most
keenly. The "sixth month" was Elul (September), the
time of year when grapes, figs, and pomegranates were
about to be harvested (Lk. 13:6-9). It was time to celebrate, but Jehovah had become weary with Jerusalem's
hypocrisy (Is. 1:13-14; 66:23).

God's message came, literally, "by the hand of" Haggai, the instrument of Jehovah. "The Word of the Lord"
began to flow through His servant like a mighty river. Our
central figure is called "the prophet" five times in this book
(Hag. 1:1,3,12; 2:1,10)—the Bible number for grace, God's
righteousness and corresponding enablement. This

word in Hebrew means "an inspired man; to speak or sing by inspiration." It's earliest use describes someone who became God's mouthpiece under the influence of the divine Spirit (1 Sam. 10:6). A prophet is one who "sees" into the invisible realm and then speaks for God to men. At this time in post-exilic Israel, Jehovah had focused His human telescope on a singular vision: the latter house of greater glory, unshakeable in the Feast of Tabernacles.

Haggai first addresses "Zerubbabel the son of Shealtiel, governor of Judah." This powerful man who led the first expedition back to Jerusalem reveals the "king" principle. "Zerubbabel" means "descended from Babylon; that is, born there; sown, conceived, born in Babylon; shoot from Babylon; begotten in confusion." He was the son of "Shealtiel," which means "I have asked God; to inquire of or demand of El." He is mentioned seven times in Haggai and 14 other times in the Old Testament (Zech. 4:6-10). Zerubbabel is honored in both Messianic genealogies (Mt. 1:12; Lk. 3:27).

Zerubbabel was the heir apparent to David's throne, the grandson of King Jehoiachin, who had been deported to Babylon in 597 B.C. (2 Kings 24:15). The genealogy of First Chronicles 3:19 states Zerubbabel to be the son of Jehoiachin's third son, Pedaiah, whereas Shealtiel, the eldest, appears to have been childless. Shealtiel had probably adopted his eldest nephew, or bore him to Pedaiah's widow by Levirate marriage. Zerubbabel's father had petitioned Jehovah that his "son," though born in strange land, be a mighty tool in the hand of God. King Cyrus had made Zerubbabel prefect or "governor";

this Aramaic word, a general term for a divisionary civil or military ruler of a kingdom, is *pechah* and could mean "protector or captain." The Persian name for this "prince of Judah" was "Sheshbazzar" (Ezra 1:8,14; 5:14,16), which means "fire worshiper; joyous vintager, joy of the vintage, unassailable joy, joy in tribulation." Thus, Haggai and Zerubbabel had kindred names and spirits whose strength was the joy of Jehovah (Neh. 8:10). The man who led the crusade back to the land, like his ancestor David, was king over "Judah," king over "praise" (2 Sam. 2:4).

Haggai next zeroes in on Joshua the son of Josedech, the high priest. This holy minister, a descendant of righteous Zadok and responsible for the ecclesiastical affairs in the Jerusalem community, reveals the "priest" principle. "Joshua" (also called Jeshua 11 times in the Book of Ezra) means "Jehovah is salvation, Jah is savior, Jehovah is deliverer; whom Jehovah makes triumphant; Jah makes rich; Jehovah is deliverance, Jehovah is help." Compare this with the names Hosea and Jesus. Joshua is mentioned five times by Haggai and six times by Zechariah. This priest was the son of "Josedech" (or Jozadak), which means "whom Jehovah makes just; righteousness of Jah, innocence of Jehovah, Jah is great." Joshua is called the "high" or "great" priest. For the etymology of the word for "priest," see the exegesis of Haggai 2:11 in Chapter Seven.

Together, Zerubbabel and Joshua prefigure the Lord Jesus Christ, the true King-Priest, who by His resurrection raised up the true temple, His Body (Jn. 2:19-22). These two men also signal the firstfruits remnant to be "kings and priests," foreshadowing the New Testament priesthood after the order of Melchisedec (Heb. 5:1-8:6; Rev. 1:6). Haggai's first words are addressed to God's delegated authority, not the people. Divine government is theocratic, not democratic. All authority is centered in Jesus, then passed to those whom He singles out. Zerubbabel and Joshua had followed the people's whims, their congregation the heathen's ways. The Jews had bred among visionless Samaritans and soon became like their worldly neighbors—weak and compromising. Bad company had corrupted good character (1 Cor. 15:33).

The leaders and citizens to whom Haggai spoke were indeed a "firstfruits" company (Jas. 1:18; Rev. 14:1-5). This term illustrates "excellent" or "threefold" things (Prov. 22:20), a basic rule of biblical hermeneutics explained in Chapter One of my book, *The More Excellent Ministry* (Shippensburg, PA: Destiny Image Publishing, 1988). A chart listing over 40 examples of "threefold" things is given in Chapter Two of a companion volume entitled, *Prevail: A Handbook for the Overcomer* (Shippensburg, PA: Destiny Image Publishers, 1982). The grandfather clause of this key principle is the divine pattern seen in Moses' Tabernacle and the corresponding Feasts of the Lord:

Outer Court	Holy Place	Most Holy Place
Passover	Pentecost	Tabernacles
Born again	Spirit-filled	Mature
Babes	Youth	Men

The principle of harvest parallels these three dimensions—the gleanings, the bulk of the harvest, and the "firstfruits." The latter matures early, forecasting the extent and quality of the upcoming crop. Who were these people? What were they like before being choked by fear and the cares of this world? The returning firstfruits company was a willing, working, and worshiping people (Ezra 1:5; 2:68; 3:3-4). God had "raised" or "awakened (by opening the eyes)" the spirit of this remnant (Ezra 1:5). This same word is used in Ezra 1:1 to express how God "stirred up" Cyrus, King of Persia (Deut. 32:11; Ps. 57:8; Is. 50:4).

A serving people is a seeing people, a community inspired with vision and understanding (Eph. 1:18). In their beginnings, divine aspiration had taken precedence over human comforts and concerns. Leaving familiar routine and walking toward uncharted territory, the ransomed pilgrims had pressed the upward call, ascending the hilly city to do Jehovah's bidding. The Church has been summoned to ascend past the common surroundings of Passover and Pentecost, to go on to maturity, to experience Zion's King, the Lord of the harvest in the Feast of Tabernacles (Phil. 3:12-14; Heb. 6:1-2). Zerubbabel, Joshua, and the people had initially arisen with great determination (Is. 35:10; 60:1; Eph. 5:14). The altar had been restored and the foundation laid. What joy, what hope and expectation in a day of new beginnings— what zeal and courage! But what happened?

Build Him a House

The people's hearts had grown cold toward spiritual things, their true condition had become camouflaged by evasion and procrastination. But there was no excuse; Persian decrees, like Jehovah's, could not be altered!

Hag. 1:2, KJV

Thus speaketh the Lord of hosts, saying, This people say, The time is not come, the time that the Lord's house should be built.

Hag. 1:2, TLB

"Why is everyone saying it is not the right time for rebuilding My Temple?" asks the Lord.

The One who longs to inhabit a people is "the Lord of hosts," or *Jehovah-Tsebaoth*, the "Lord of the armies" of heaven and earth. He is so named 14 times by Haggai, 53 times by Zechariah, and 24 times by Malachi. This divine name appears over 300 times, mostly in the prophetic books; its first mention is First Samuel 1:3. These "heavenly armies" were symbolized by the golden cherubim that covered the Ark of the Covenant, between which the "Lord of hosts" was enthroned (1 Sam. 4:4). From David's time, there had been a particular link between this sacred title and Jerusalem, "the city of the Lord of hosts" (Ps. 48:8). *Jehovah-Tsebaoth* may have been His temple name (Ps. 24).

Father God asks, "Where is My House? Where is My army? Where is your desire for My vision and heart?" Sadly, He addresses the remnant as "this" people, not "My" people. The word for "people" in Haggai 1:2 means "a congregated unit; a tribe or flock." A singular frame of mind had infiltrated the Jerusalem community (Amos 3:3). They literally said, "It is not time to come..." The root word for "time" means "to advance; to pass on or to continue." The halting remnant had adopted the

Samaritan lifestyle, dug in their heels, and refused to go any further.

The "Lord's house" in verse two is a habitation for God, not man (1 Chron. 29:1; Ezra 1:2). The "mansion" or "dwelling place" of John 14:2 is the New Testament Temple where the Spirit of the Father and the Son take up residence and come to "abide" (Jn. 14:23). God's sole project in the earth is to create for Himself a permanent dwelling in the hearts and lives of His people. The Hebrew word for "house" in Haggai 1:2 is *bayith* (Strong's #1004), an abbreviated form of *banah*, the word for "built" in the same verse. The Lord's "House" is mentioned seven times in Haggai's prophecy (1:2,4,8,14; 2:3,7,9)—the Bible number for perfection or completion? The New Testament word for "house" (*oikos*) means "a residence, abode, dwelling; by implication, a family." In the New Covenant, the "House" of the Lord has five applications:

1. *Jesus Himself, the House of the Father (see Jn. 1:14; 14:2,11; Col. 1:19; 2:9).*

2. *The individual believer (Mt. 7:24; 12:29; 2 Cor. 5:1-2).*

3. *The home and family (see Acts 2:46; 5:42; 16:31; 1 Cor. 16:15; Heb. 11:7).*

4. *The local church (see Mt. 5:15; Mk. 3:25; Col. 4:15; 1 Tim. 3:15; 1 Pet. 4:17).*

5. *The household of faith, the Body of Christ (see Gal. 6:10; Eph. 2:19; 2 Tim. 2:20; Heb. 3:6; 10:21; 1 Pet. 2:5).*

The Finished Temple Is an Undivided Heart

The "temple" is mentioned but twice in the Book of Haggai (Hag. 2:15,18). Zerubbabel's temple was known in Jewish terminology as "the second temple" and was never replaced by a third. The temple rebuilt by Herod the Great in the days of Jesus was considered to be simply a refurbishing. The purpose of unshakeable peace is to finish the sanctuary, to save the whole man. To comprehend the scope of this principle, one must be acquainted with the several temples or tabernacles mentioned throughout the Scriptures:

1. *The tabernacle in the wilderness (Ex. 25–40).*

2. *The tabernacle of David (2 Sam. 6; 1 Chron. 13–17).*

3. *The temple of Solomon (1 Kings 5–9; 1 Chron. 1–7).*

4. *The temple of Zerubbabel (Ezra 1–6; Hag. 1–2).*

5. *The temple of Ezekiel's vision (Ezek. 40–48).*

6. *The temple of Herod (Jn. 2:20).*

7. *The temple of God in Jesus Christ (Jn. 2:19-22).*

8. *The temple of the Holy Spirit, individually and corporately (1 Cor. 6:19; Eph. 2:21).*

The Hebrew word for "temple" is *heykal* (Strong's #1964) and means (in the sense of capacity) "a large public building, such as a palace or temple." *Vine's Expository Dictionary of Biblical Words* adds, "a large house" (Thomas Nelson Publishers, 1985). Used 78 times in the Old Testament (mostly in Ezekiel), it is first mentioned in First Samuel 1:9 and 3:3. It occurs frequently in the

Book of Psalms (see Ps. 11:4; 27:4; 65:4; 68:29; 138:2). See also Zechariah 6:12-15; 8:9, and Malachi 3:1. The most common expressions in the King James Version are the temple "of the Lord" or His "holy" temple. There are two New Testament words for "temple":

1. *heiron*—*the physical temple in Jerusalem.*

2. *naos*—*the spiritual temple, Jesus and His Church.*

Heiron is used throughout the Gospels, the Book of Acts, and First Corinthians 9:13 to describe the literal building, the natural temple at Jerusalem. This word is #2411 in Strong's and means "a sacred place (the entire precincts) of the temple (at Jerusalem or elsewhere)." *Naos*, the spiritual building, the real temple, pertains to the Lord Jesus Christ and His Body, the Church. It is #3485 in Strong's Concordance and means "a fane, shrine, or temple." The *naos* of God is the "inner sanctuary," taken from the primary word *naio* (to dwell). The word *fane* is from the Latin *fanum* (a sanctuary or temple) and *fari* (to speak, consecrate) and means "a temple or church."

First, *naos* pertains to the temple of God in Christ Jesus, the One who came from the heart or bosom of the Father (Mk. 14:58; Jn. 2:19-21).

Rev. 21:22, KJV

And I saw no temple therein: for the Lord God Almighty and the Lamb are the temple of it.

Second, *naos* refers to the temple of God, the Church (see 1 Cor. 6:19; 2 Cor. 6:16; Eph. 2:21; 2 Thess. 2:4). This word is used in all 16 references for "temple" found in the Book of Revelation. This is the house, the people, the spiritual family that Father God desires to assemble, restore and fill with His glory and unending peace. *Naos*, the "inner sanctuary," is the true temple, the Most Holy Place, the spirit of man—his heart.

1 Cor. 3:16-17, NIV

> *Don't you know that you yourselves are God's temple and that God's Spirit lives in you? If anyone destroys God's temple, God will destroy him; for God's temple is sacred, and you are that temple.*

Haggai constantly challenges us to be involved with a work that contains God's desire. The first step in that direction is to understand that the finished temple is an undivided heart completely devoted to the Lord. Our lives are to be a whole burnt offering, a living sacrifice (Ps. 51:19). All creation groans for His Body to be full of light and life (Mt. 6:22; Rom. 8:22). Jehovah wanted the remnant's full attention, their "whole heart" (Ps. 119:10,34,58,69,145). The purpose of unshakeable peace is to save the whole man: heart, mind, and body. The endtime Body of Christ is putting on the whole armor (Eph. 6:11). Jesus, the heavenly Zerubbabel, will complete the temple and build His Church; His Spirit will enable us to give the undivided affection of our "whole heart" (Jer. 24:7).

Build a Son

The word for "built" here in Haggai 1:2 is *banah* (Strong's #1129) and means "to build or rebuild." Its noun form is *ben*, the Hebrew word for "son." As noted above, the word for "house" in this verse is an abbreviated form of *banah*. The heavenly Father's ultimate intention is to fashion and build a many-membered *son*, a corporate man after His own heart who will do His will (Acts 13:22). The new creation man is the New Testament house of the Lord, a habitation of God through the Spirit. His temple is a family of sons. Paradoxically, this glorious Body is also the Bride of Christ (Eph. 5:22-33), His heavenly companion of like nature and ability. The glorious Church is an ongoing incarnation, built together and growing unto a holy temple in the Lord (Jn. 1:12; Eph. 2:21-22).

Gal. 4:19, KJV

> *My little children, of whom I travail in birth again until Christ be formed in you.*

Simply stated, the finishing of Zerubbabel's temple prefigures the formation of Christ in His Body as set forth in John 17, Romans 8, First Corinthians 12–13, Ephesians 4, and Hebrews 10. This many-membered son is the full-grown Church, the finished sanctuary, a manchild fully formed within His Bride (Rev. 12:5). The firstborn Son that bruised satan's head is the prototype of that glorious company of mature brethren who will follow their Forerunner into the holiest of all, there to fully appropriate His life and victory (Gen. 3:15; Rom. 16:20; Heb. 6:19-20). The fivefold ascension gift ministries are the team of architects through whom the Lord Jesus has determined to complete His house (1 Cor. 3:10; Eph. 4:11-13). They are the "tutors and governors" who discipline and train the Heir in the ways of the Father (Gal. 4:1-7; Heb. 12:5-11).

The heavenly Dove flew the Pentecostal coop in the 1960s and 1970s; the Holy Spirit was poured out on every denomination. Men and women, even preachers and priests, forsook the religious confusion of Babylon's systems and traditions (Mk. 7:13). The altar of prayer and worship was built into their lives; the teachers of the 70's made sure that the foundations, the first principles, were laid (Heb. 6:1-2). Depending upon the reader, that period was thirty, twenty, or fifteen years ago, perhaps even ten years ago...five years ago.

The Person who called you has never changed (Heb. 13:8). The promise that thrilled you has never changed (1 Kings 8:56). The power that will enable you to finish your course with joy has never changed (Phil. 1:6). God has never changed. His heart and purpose for His people remains the same. What has happened to us?

A Life Style of Neglect

Haggai's message addresses a tremendous need in our generation. In the mad pursuit of our personal agendas, we have abandoned the true purpose of God in the earth. Locally and universally, He is adjusting our priorities, calling us back to finish His work. God's primary vision had been delayed for fifteen years: Not much was happening over at His house, no real spiritual operation. Haggai's congregation considered this inactivity to be Jehovah's responsibility, that He had suspended His plans for a season. God is not in limbo. His Spirit has been on the move since Genesis 1:2. The problem is not the lack of divine desire to work, but the lack of human desire to be used! A subtle influence had settled into the remnant. The ruined, devastated condition of Zerubbabel's temple had overwhelmed the people. In the enormity of the task, they had lost heart for His work.

Has neglect become your spiritual posture? Has your disregard for God's House caused you to justify an accustomed way of life by declaring that this is not the season...that the day of true revival is over? Have you lost your passion for Him and His purpose?

Forty-five years have passed since the Latter Rain outpouring (1948-1956), yet we are still surrounded by a great need to see His house finished, the glorious Church come to maturity. Our lives are besieged by the daily challenge of an incomplete temple; we have divided affections. Only a real word from God can break the bands of our spiritually devastated condition and raise our hope from the dead. Men pray, "Lord, give us a fresh glory. Let it return and fill Your House." But He replies, "I don't have a house! All men seek to build their own houses while My sanctuary lies waste. You are praying for My glory to fill something that is incomplete and inadequate."

Some reminisce over the glory of the good old days, but we want more than stories of yesteryear (Hag. 2:3). We expect to witness a generational move of God for ourselves and our children. Because the cloud of real revival has not come, men have begun to faint. We pray, "Lord, when Your glory comes, Your Church will arise and begin to function." No! His glory will never alight upon the Body in its present spiritual temperature and condition. We proclaim the message of Tabernacles while yet we are Pentecostal in life style—in part and imperfect. The fullness of divine glory can only be poured into a finished work, not an old bottle (Ex. 40:33-38; 2 Chron. 5:1,12-14; Jn. 17:4-5).

The *purpose* of enduring peace is to complete the temple, to save the whole man. That can only happen in the context of corporate vision—the big picture. Disjointed bones in the valley need to be reactivated, reconnected to one another and the Lord (Ezek. 37:11). Our life style has killed our desire to be His extended hand. Men complain, "There's little happening over at the house of the Lord to motivate my involvement." But the real dilemma is that no one is ready to accommodate what God wants! Our capacity, our heart and vision, is limited and small. The way we live does not permit the unrestricted availability of reckless faith, an abandonment to do His will. We have cluttered our lives—our homes, our churches, our ministries—with the "rubbish" of this world. This word means "dust; clay, earth, mud; clods, ashes" (Neh. 4:10). The first man, Adam, is a man of dust, earth-minded. We are called to put on and wear the image of Christ (Gen. 2:7; 1 Cor. 15:44-49).

Open up to God again. Let Him renew your aspiration to go on, to be reconnected to His heart. He desires to pour new life on wrecked and spoiled situations—the true state of most men's lives. Only God can resurrect a desire for the things of the Spirit. Repent from asking amiss. The Greek word for "neglect" in Matthew 18:17 means "to mishear, to hear amiss or imperfectly, to hear without taking heed; by implication, to disobey." Awake to the reality of another feast beyond Passover and Pentecost—a further word, a higher call. A different Greek word for "neglect" is used in First Timothy 4:14 and Hebrews 2:3-4; 8:9 and means "to be careless; not to regard." Some foolishly discount what apostles and prophets are saying, drawing back rather than drawing near (Heb. 10:19-22,38-39). God is preparing and renovating true spiritual motivation. It's training time for reigning time. Don't be negligent (2 Chron. 29:11).

Ceiled Houses

Hag. 1:3-4, KJV

> *Then came the word of the Lord by Haggai the prophet, saying, Is it time for you, O ye, to dwell in your ceiled houses, and this house lie waste?*

Hag. 1:4, NIV

> *"Is it a time for you yourselves to be living in your paneled houses, while this house remains a ruin?"*

Hag. 1:4, TLB

> *"Is it then the right time for you to live in luxurious homes, when the Temple lies in ruins?"*

The evident breach between the remnant and Jehovah is emphasized by the repetition of the personal pronoun in the original text ("you, you yourselves" [NIV]). Haggai turns the very words of the people (Hag. 1:2) back into their ears. The proper or fit time is always "today" (2 Cor. 6:2; Heb. 3:7-15; 4:7). Jehovah's prophet exposed the insincerity of their alibis; houses wainscoted with cedar were the residences of kings. It is possible that the prophet could be referring only to the governor's estate.

If so, this helps to explain why he addressed Zerubbabel first and provides a sobering lesson for every preacher. The remnant was comfortable, at ease, in Zion. They had left God without a dwelling place, while they themselves lived in costly and magnificently decorated homes. Their life style had become like that of wicked King Jehoiakim, the man who destroyed Jeremiah's scroll (Jer. 22:13-19).

The word for "dwell" in Haggai 1:4 means "to remain; to settle, to marry." Haggai's congregation was tied to its apathy, each settling for his own way. Like Achan in the Book of Joshua, the post-exilic Jews had taken what belonged to God and lavished it upon themselves, importing expensive timber only to seize it for their own use. Are we any different? We run from conference to conference, from teacher to teacher. The vision for real evangelism and a mature Church has shriveled and died while the seed lay rotting in the barn. Many have married the world. Too many of our kids look and act like Samaritans.

The word for "ceiled" houses in verse 4 is *caphan* (Strong's #5603) and means "to hide by covering; to roof in or wainscot; figuratively, to reserve." Ceiled houses are houses whose walls and ceilings were expensively inlaid with costly woodwork, as was Solomon's Temple (1 Kings 6:9; 7:3,7). The remnant had built their own "porch of judgment," privately interpreting the vision of God. Haggai's community, numb to their true spiritual condition, had defrauded God and snubbed His vision (1 Tim. 6:10). Their heathen neighbors had obliged Cyrus' request with a liberal supply of silver, gold, and other gifts, but they would do nothing for God's house. The remnant had gradually become satisfied to worship among ruins while dwelling in sumptuous homes. What shameful avarice! The returned exiles were urging poverty as the reason for their procrastination, but the prophet immediately stripped away their artificial facade. How unlike their famous forefather David (Ps. 132:1-5)!

The holy tithe or tenth of each man's income is legally the Lord's (Lev. 27:30). In most American churches, about 25 or 30 percent of the people are consistent tithers. The rest are thieves and robbers who drive around in "stolen" vehicles paid for with God's money (Mal. 3:8-10). Jesus clearly taught that one cannot serve God and mammon (Mt. 6:24). The prophet Isaiah vividly details the present plight and empty future of those who put their finances ahead of the Kingdom of God:

Is. 5:8-13, NIV

Woe to you who add house to house and join field to field till no space is left and you live alone in the land.

The Lord Almighty has declared in my hearing: "Surely the great houses will become desolate, the fine mansions left without occupants.

A ten-acre vineyard will produce only a bath of wine, a homer of seed only an ephah of grain."

Woe to those who rise early in the morning to run after their drinks, who stay up late at night till they are inflamed with wine.

They have harps and lyres at their banquets, tambourines and flutes and wine, but they have no regard for the deeds of the Lord, no respect for the work of His hands.

Therefore My people will go into exile for lack of understanding; their men of rank will die of hunger and their masses will be parched with thirst.

Does this describe your life or business? Your church or ministry? Your denomination? Then consider your ways.

Note the contrast between "your houses" and "this House" in Haggai 1:4. The desires and designs of men are plural, but the ultimate intention of the Lord is singular (2 Cor. 11:3). Because each ran to his own private life, the house of the Lord lay "waste," or "parched," "ruined." This primitive verb means "to parch (through drought); to desolate, destroy, kill." This same word is repeated in Haggai 1:9 and Nehemiah 2:3,17 to describe the condition of Jerusalem. Another prophet used the same expression while anticipating better days to come (Ezek. 36:35,38).

Walled Cities

John Calvin once said, "Men are very ingenious when they wish to hide their delinquencies." A *ceiled* house is a sealed house, a walled city. It is a false face, a man-made veneer, a clever disguise; it is a religious covering, a self-righteous tapestry, a veil of flesh that must be rent from top to bottom. A *paneled* house is the place of human reasoning, the cocoon of rationalization, the dark soulish cave where men hide to save their face from the face of the Lamb. It is the place where men do not have to change, where man is god, and gods are invented to serve the king of self. These pseudo-coverings are plastic partitions, futile attempts to build permanent things with that which is passing away. Broken, dysfunctional relationships are the sad consequence of settling in ceiled houses—lives, homes, churches, cities, and nations that are completely out of order. Chapter Four of my book, *The More Excellent Ministry*, details a priestly ministry without walls. There we noted ten areas that break covenant and disturb the peace (*The More Excellent Ministry*, 142):

1. *Walls between an individual and Jesus.*

2. *Walls between a local church and Jesus.*

3. *Walls between a husband and wife.*

4. *Walls between a parent and child.*

5. *Walls between an employer and employee.*

6. *Walls between sheep, or between shepherd and sheep.*

7. *Walls between shepherds.*

8. *Walls between local churches.*

9. *Walls between local areas.*

10. *Walls between nations.*

The Hebrew word for "wall" means "a place of protection." Walled cities are also called "fenced" cities, places that are "isolated, inaccessible by height or fortification." These little foxes can become giants (Deut. 1:28; Song 2:15). Haggai was God's war cry against Judah's lofty pride.

The remnant were taken up with their personal lives, conveniently shutting out Jehovah's plans. The prophetic rebuke battered against their uncaring frame of mind. The Prophet Christ Jesus, the "Ram" for the burnt offering (Gen. 22:13), has torn down every wall to provide abiding peace. His trumpets, the prophets, are crying against every high thing that disturbs His glory (Zeph. 1:16).

Eph. 2:14, AMP

...and has broken down (destroyed, abolished) the hostile dividing wall between us.

The Greek word for "wall" in this verse is *phragmos* (Strong's # 5418) which means "a fence, or inclosing barrier." It is taken from *phrasso*, which means "to block up, to silence, to stop." Luke's Gospel mentions the "hedges," (Lk. 14:23) places where men seclude themselves in "ceiled" houses. There we exist, absent of real revival, our pride refusing to acknowledge obvious deficiencies. We play hide-and-seek behind the custom-designed walls of private utopias. There we safely cloister, camouflaged in an attempt to avoid God and His prophet, indisposed to face the reality of a sanctuary cluttered with spiritual trash. Man-made walls are mudded together with pride and conceit—the product of a blinded mind (Prov. 18:11; 2 Cor. 4:1-4). Religious spirits feed a fierce independence that refuses to acknowledge God's greater purpose: the completion of the Body of Christ in the Most Holy Place.

When God decides to dismantle the places where men hide from His will, He sends a prophet. Habakkuk predicted that the stones and beams of these religious structures would cry out for vengeance in the day of the

Lord (Hab. 2:11-12). The writing is on the wall; Babylon's days are numbered (Dan. 5:5); the Word is digging us (Ezek. 8:7-10); God's prophetic army is arising (Joel 2:7-11); no wall is too high (Ps. 18:29); a soon-coming shout of faith is about to bring down every high thing within and without that exalts itself against the knowledge of God (Josh. 6:20; 2 Cor. 10:4-5).

Do the First Works

Rev. 2:4, KJV

Nevertheless I have somewhat against thee, because thou hast left thy first love.

Remember therefore from whence thou art fallen, and repent, and do the first works....

Materialism, the love of money, is only part of our difficulty. Up till now, we have neglected the operation of the Holy Ghost. Called out of Babylon to recover the house of the Lord, we have spurned our first love. The number one obstacle to His plan of restoration is the current preoccupation of God's people to build their own private lives! We must be delivered from personal agendas unto a corporate mindset, from "I, me, mine" to "we, us." We are out of focus. The American dream is not the high calling (Phil. 3:14). Houses and lands, the lower realms of ease, compromise, and personal comfort are private havens designed to shield us from the reality of our spiritual devastation. Men get involved in all kinds of things because they cannot face the real condition of their hearts. Our toys vary, but we manage to stay busy dodging the truth.

Real prophets who zoom in on the Church's true situation are hated men. Haggai confronted this predicament head-on by getting into the face of a self-righteous remnant and exposing their motives. Each had said, "I will spare no expense to fabricate a house of ease that harbors me from admitting the collapse and decay of the house of the Lord." Every man is partially responsible for this corporate downfall. Each person must repent, reconnect, and do his "first works" again. Stir up your gift and go back to work.

Some men have become sidetracked with expensive building programs. Truth is ignored while, like Solomon, they keep a full schedule building bigger barns—outward manifestations of what they lack inwardly (Eccles. 2:4-11; Lk. 12:16-21). There was no living water or fruit within the wise man, so he built pools and gardens. His empty heart had no song like his famous father's, so he hired quartets and choirs.

This is but one way men have been creating a different definition of God's designs and purposes. Great individuals are seeking their own fulfillment, but their projects are inadequate and inappropriate. The flesh has been unleashed in its inordinate ambition to build something great to the glory of God. Men construct literal houses while the real building, comprised of burnt stones charred by neglect, still lies broken in a heap of ashes.

Reattach to the true Vine, refocus upon the divine objective. With renewed courage and passion, we can revolutionize the present condition. God is sending a fresh outpouring of the Holy Spirit to do the work (Zech. 4:6). Men's hearts have become hard and calloused. The present phenomena of "holy laughter" and uninhibited joy will help break up our fallow ground (Jer. 4:3; Hos. 10:12). Isaac ("laughter"), the son of promise, is being born, preparing us for the glory of the third feast. As with every other genuine manifestation, this is being parroted and prostituted, but we need to understand that:

1. *Holy laughter is therapeutic. "A merry heart doeth good like a medicine" (Prov. 17:22a). We need to be healed.*

2. *Holy laughter is preparing a people heretofore ignorant of anything supernatural to participate in an outpouring of the Spirit that cannot be explained or controlled by men. Laughter can be a symbol for conquest (Ps. 2:4). We must abandon ourselves to Him.*

The Samaritans

To fully grasp the prophet's rebuke, we need to review the actual circumstances that caused the temple project work to cease. The adversaries of Judah and Benjamin were the Samaritans, a mongrel race with foreign blood and false worship—"gods of their own" (2 Kings 17:24-29). The Jewish historian Josephus describes them as opportunists. When the Jews enjoyed prosperity (the money that came from Cyrus' decree), these compromisers were quick to acknowledge their blood relationship. The Hebrew root word for "Samaritan" is *shamar* (Strong's #8104) and means "to hedge about with thorns." These enemies to God's purpose were messengers of satan, typified by the heathen king of Ezra 4 (2 Cor. 12:7).

Ezra 4:4, KJV

Then the people of the land weakened the hands of the people of Judah, and troubled them in building,

And hired counsellors against them, to frustrate their purpose, all the days of Cyrus king of Persia, even until the reign of Darius king of Persia.

And in the reign of Ahasuerus, in the beginning of his reign, wrote they unto him an accusation against the inhabitants of Judah and Jerusalem.

And in the days of Artaxerxes wrote Bishlam, Mithredath, Tabeel, and the rest of their companions, unto Artaxerxes king of Persia; and the writing of the letter was written in the Syrian tongue, and interpreted in the Syrian tongue.

The Samaritans "weakened" or "slackened" the hands of Judah. The Living Bible says that "the local residents tried to discourage and frighten them by sending agents to tell lies about them..." (Ezra 4:4 TLB). They "troubled" or "alarmed and agitated" the Jews in building, and they temporarily hired counselors to "frustrate," and to "break up or violate" their purpose. The primary ploy of Judah's enemies was to write a letter of accusation, literally, "an attacking letter" against the Jews, to the king. According to Ezra 4:7, one has to be heathen to write or receive (interpret) such a letter! The righteous remnant, destined for never-failing peace, have closed the tablet of their hearts to this kind of devilish slander. In the New Testament, satan is the god and prince of this world system, the "accuser" of the brethren (Jn. 12:31; 2 Cor. 4:4; Rev. 12:10). This Greek word means "against one in the assembly; a complaintant at law," and its root expresses a public accusation (Jn. 8:10).

Samaritans, like Ishmael, always persecute the son of promise (Gen. 21:9; Gal. 4:29). They are adversaries of Judah (praise) and Benjamin (sonship). Samaritans turn up in many forms: angry religious systems, angry people, angry attitudes, angry thoughts, evil spirits. These "adversaries" to the purpose of unbreakable relationships are of their father the devil. Jesus adds and multiplies; satan subtracts and divides. The Samaritan opposition reveals the mystery of iniquity and lawlessness. True worshippers, a throne-room kind of people, always upset religious spirits. Samaritans get together every time Joshua (Jesus) invades their land. This same spirit was in the crowd that killed Jesus and imprisoned the early apostles. Ezra 4:7-10 describes their confederation and political covenant-making in the name of status quo. Samaritans despise change!

Ezra 4:13,16, KJV

> *Be it known now unto the king, that, if this city be builded, and the walls set up again, then will they not pay toll, tribute, and custom, and so thou shalt endamage the revenue of the kings.*
>
> *We certify the king that, if this city be builded again, and the walls thereof set up, by this means thou shalt have no portion on this side the river.*

The other side of the river represents the invisible realm. "This side" of the river (the veil) is the visible realm.

Every significant happening in Ezra 4-6 was based upon what had been written on the other side of the river. The decree of a sovereign God is His predetermined counsel. If we can rediscover His edict in the volume of the Book, it's a done deal! There can be no work without a word.

The devil knows that the restored Church will do damage to his royal revenue (Mt. 16:18; Rom. 16:20). Once we become the habitation of God through the Spirit, the adversary cannot exact tribute from our lives. Our time, talent, and tithe will once again belong to the Lord. There will be no more "toll"; we'll spend our money on God and not the devil and his crowd. There the will be no more "tribute"; we'll stop singing satan's praises in our music and preaching. There will be no more "custom"; there will be no Halloween, Christmas, and Easter in the unshakeable Kingdom. Ultimately, the prince of this world will have no "portion" or "part; allotment; inheritance" of this side of the river, this veil of flesh (Neh. 2:20; Jn. 14:30). The latter house of greater glory will rid the earth of the influence of satan. Even his memory will perish (Neh. 2:20; Is. 26:13-14)!

Ezra 4:23, KJV

Now when the copy of king Artaxerxes' letter was read before Rehum, and Shimshai the scribe, and their companions, they went up in haste to Jerusalem unto the Jews, and made them to cease by force and power.

Have you ever received a nasty letter from the devil or his crowd? Trashy mail, political fliers, are found throughout the Old Testament (see 2 Sam. 11:15; 1 Kings

21:8; 2 Kings 19:14; Neh. 6:19; Esther 3:13; 8:5) and the New Testament (Acts 9:2; 2 Thess. 2:2). Put them in file 13, the Bible number for rebellion. Run them through the shredder of the anointed Word or send them to the dead letter office! These lies are powerless against peacemakers determined to become God's dwelling-place.

The Jews were completely intimidated by the Samaritan confederacy, a religious spirit of fear. It took a lot to stop the remnant, but the work on the temple was made to cease, literally, by "power" and "a strong army." (Ezra 4:23) Take courage, child of God; you cannot be defeated. You may be discouraged. Most likely, you are only distracted. The serpent is nipping at your heels. He wants to keep you off balance, disconnected, insecure. The devil is beelzebub, just a fly in your face. It's time for re-establishment, to get back to work, and to get reconnected to the House of the Lord. Rekindle Jesus' original vision for your life, your marriage, your business, your ministry. The King's decree has gone forth: "Build God's house!"

Bury the past. It's a new day. Consider your ways. Ask for forgiveness and a new heart. Receive Haggai's *rebuke*. He is about to give you the divine *remedy*.

Chapter Three

The Remedy

"Go up to the mountain, and bring wood…"

Haggai 1:5-11

The greatest enemy of faith and hope is an un-criticized present. Jehovah's swift *rebuke* settled down over the dusty ruins of an unfinished habitation, exposing every excuse. The remnant's days of hiding in a covered house was over. Such bold preaching had not been heard in years, but Haggai's backbone came from the joy of the Lord (Neh. 8:10). Zerubbabel and Joshua were great men who had allowed their courage to smolder like flax, smothered by the political correctness of majority rule. They had fallen short, stumbling up the rocky path to Zion.

Consider Your Ways

Haggai challenged his compatriots to review their experience, to account for their poverty-stricken condition and meager harvest. Disillusionment and weariness had replaced the exhilarating sense of adventure that once marked their spiritual beginnings. Haggai's first words had been directed to the governor and the high priest (Hag. 1:1-4). But from verse four onward, it becomes very clear that every man is to consider his ways.

Hag. 1:5, KJV

Now therefore thus saith the Lord of hosts; Consider your ways.

Hag. 1:5, NIV
...Give careful thought to your ways.

Hag. 1:5, TLB

Look at the result.

Hag. 1:5, JB

So now, Yahweh Sabaoth says this: Reflect carefully how things have gone for you....

"Now" means "at this time." Haggai used the very words of the people's excuse to declare that it was indeed the time to build again (Hag. 1:2). The "Lord of hosts" begins to administer His antidote for their spiritual infirmity. First, they were to "consider" their ways. Mentioned five times in the Book of Haggai (1:5,7; 2:10,18 [twice]), this reprimand is a combination of three Hebrew words:

1. *Strong's #7760—suwm, "To put, place, set, or fix."*

2. *Strong's #3820—leb, "The heart; the intellect, feelings, or will; the center of anything."*

3. *Strong's #5921—'al, "Above, over, upon, or against."*

Jehovah-Tsebaoth was plainly saying, "Set your heart upon your ways, then center your heart back upon My ways!" The Jews were to examine themselves and return their hearts to the project that contained His (1 Cor. 11:28). Have you considered the great things the Lord has done for you (2 Sam. 12:24)? It's time to "fix our heart upon" God's will, to reconsider the work of His hands (Is. 5:12; Dan. 9:23). Many only want to have a good time, to overdose on a man-centered gospel. Like fleshly Esau, they want covenant with God on their own terms. We should praise Him on the instruments and enjoy the wine of His Spirit…but what about the work of the Lord, His plan in the earth?

The parallel Greek word for "consider" is *katanoeo* (Strong's #2657) and means "to observe fully." *Vine's* adds, "to perceive clearly, to understand fully, to consider closely" (Lk. 12:24,27; Heb. 3:1; 10:24). In the King James Version it is translated as "behold, consider, discover, perceive." Haggai's community had immigrated from Babylon for a better country, then allowed worldly mixture to consume their spiritual zeal (Heb. 11:14-16). Apprehended ones embrace the Lord with the same intensity with which He has embraced them. Those who attempt the work of God in their own wisdom and strength eventually faint (Ps. 127:1; Heb. 12:3).

The redeemed people had meandered from Jehovah's path. The word for ways in Haggai 1:5 is *derek* (Strong's #1870) and means "a road (as trodden); figuratively, a course of life or mode of action." Occurring over 700 times in biblical Hebrew, this word is translated in the King James Version as "conversation, custom, journey, and manner." *Vine's* adds that *derek* means "way (path, road, highway); distance; journey; manner, conduct; condition; destiny." The Church of the firstborn is returning to the center of the road (Jn. 14:6). The distance between past captivity and present restoration is the stretch of highway between two feasts, Pentecost and Tabernacles. Active change in life style happens when we turn back to His power and rule—His "way" (see Ps. 37:5; Prov. 3:5-6; Is. 55:8-9; Rev. 15:3).

The Greek equivalent is *hodos* (Strong's #3598) and means "a road; by implication, a progress (the route, act, or distance); figuratively, a mode or means." *Vine's* adds, "a natural path, road, way; metaphorically, of a course of conduct or a way of thinking." The Church is at the crossroads where two "ways" meet (Mk. 11:4). The prophetic ministry has gone ahead to prepare His "ways." Many are closing their ears to His voice, determined to follow the "ways" of tradition (Mt. 22:5; Lk. 1:76). Like the ten faithless spies dispatched by Moses, they are intimidated by giants of dispensationalism and walled cities of religious routine (Hos 14:9).

Present truth must be birthed in one's heart by the Holy Spirit, who alone understands the "ways" of righteousness (Acts 2:28; 13:10). He stewards that revelation through apostles and prophets, Spirit-led men whose "ways" are in Christ, gifts from Jesus to His Church (see 1 Cor. 4:17; Eph. 2:20; 3:5; 4:11). Though miracles abound and men see His acts, few know His "ways" (Ps. 103:7; Mt. 7:13-14; Heb. 3:10). The double-minded emphasize the devil and the old man more than our victorious King and the new creation in His image. But the "ways" into the Most Holy Place has been consecrated by the blood of the Lamb (Mt. 3:3; Acts 18:26; Heb. 10:19-22)! While Pharaoh retreats to the house of hardened hearts, God is turning our spirits back toward His paths (Ex. 7:23). Brethren, it's time to declare the word of release, to return to the "ways" of the Lord (Ps. 138:5; Ezek. 40:4).

Much Is Little

Hag. 1:6, KJV

Ye have sown much, and bring in little; ye eat, but ye have not enough; ye drink, but ye are not filled with drink; ye clothe you, but there is none warm; and he that earneth wages earneth wages to put it into a bag with holes.

Hag. 1:6, TLB

You plant much but harvest little. You have scarcely enough to eat or drink, and not enough clothes to keep you warm. Your income disappears, as though you were putting it into pockets filled with holes!

The divine *remedy* continues. To be healed and restored, the remnant must become "poor in spirit" and acknowledge their need (Mt. 5:3). God's people had been sowing much, only to store it in a torn purse, a bag with holes. True spirituality is not to be measured by one's accumulation of natural wealth or Scriptural knowledge. Haggai's remnant church had reaped little; it was hungry, thirsty, naked, and poor (Rev. 3:17). The word for "sown" in verse six means "to sow; figuratively, to dis-seminate, plant, fructify; to make pregnant." It is found in Psalm 126:5, Ecclesiastes 11:4,6, Isaiah 32:20, 55:10, Hosea 8:7, and Micah 6:15.

The word for "much" means "increase; to multiply, become numerous, become great." It reveals the heart motive of religious sectarianism: numbers—the size of the crowd and the offering. Men still want to build towers and make a name for themselves (Gen. 11:4). The word for "bring in" means to "come in or enter in," and refers to the harvest. Abundant sowing had produced sparingly (Is. 5:8-10). In New Covenant reality, the full crop will not "enter" the barn until we come into sabbath rest within the veil (Heb. 4:1-9; 6:19-20). The fields had yielded "little," literally, "small or few." Little is much when God is in it. Much is little when man is in charge. The Almighty is not impressed with our stack of num-bers. We should weigh, not count the saints, measuring them on scales of glory (2 Cor. 4:17-18; 10:12).

Every doctrinal stream has its own golden calf. Leaders everywhere have intermingled two visions, two agendas, two seeds: what the Lord wants and what the people want (Deut. 22:9). Each has crafted a god to his own liking and denominational image—one that con-dones current whims. Each man attends his own church and worships the Jesus of his choice, customarily proclaimed by his favorite preacher (1 Cor. 3:1-4). We have fished all night but caught nothing. We have carried much seed and brought in little, spending our strength in vain. We are barren and embarrassed (Lev. 26:19-20; Deut. 28:38; Ps. 107:34).

Jer. 14:4, KJV

...the plowmen were ashamed, they covered their heads.

Amos 4:6, NIV

"I gave you empty stomachs in every city and lack of bread in every town...."

"Ye eat, but ye have not enough..." The word for "eat" in Haggai 1:6 means "to eat, feed, consume, devour." The word for "enough" speaks of that which satisfies and suffices. Seminars, conventions, books, cassette tapes, videos...ad nauseum: we have swallowed anything and everything, but it's not *enough*. Our upgraded data banks are loaded with all sorts of information, but we have not returned to the Lord. The young prodigal in Luke 15 feasted on the empty "husks" of a previous move of God; his dinner companions were content to eat the leftovers of yesterday's feast.

The remnant had played the harlot, lusting after their own comfort rather than heeding God's plan (Hos. 4:10). Idolatry had taken them captive for 70 long years...would they ever learn (2 Tim. 3:5-7)? Christians are starving for the meat of the Word. In days of famine, men are forced to eat ass's head (2 Kings 6:20): human wisdom without God—the anointing replaced by academics and demographics. It comes with a side dish of dove's dung—what is left of the dove after he has flown away! Ichabod...the glory has departed. The Holy Spirit will not light upon dead flesh (Gen. 8:9)—men or movements that refuse to hear His prophets.

Ezek. 4:16, NIV

He then said to me: "Son of man, I will cut off the supply of food in Jerusalem. The people will eat rationed food in anxiety and drink rationed water in despair."

"Ye drink, but ye are not filled with drink" (Hag. 1:6c). The word for "drink" in verse six means "to imbibe," and it is sometimes translated as "banquet" in the King James Version. "Filled with drink" means "to become tipsy; to satiate with a stimulating drink or influence." The "banqueting house" of Song of Solomon 2:4 is the "house of wine." Passover feast marked our godly beginnings (Ex. 12:2). Pentecost is the subsequent feast of joy and laughter. Though delivered by blood, water, and Spirit (1 Cor. 10:1-4; 1 Jn. 5:8), we thirst for more, having inherited a well that does not fully satisfy (Is. 5:13; Lam. 4:4; Jn. 4:13). The essence of true worship is total sacrifice (Gen. 22:5). Theologically, Heaven's Lamb died on the cross as God thirsting for man and man thirsting for God (Ps. 69:21; Jn. 19:28). Jesus, whose sole determination was to be the Father's house, is the Water of life. He alone can slake our thirst (see Mt. 5:6; Jn. 4:14; 6:35; 7:37).

Amos 8:13, NIV

In that day the lovely young women and strong young men will faint because of thirst.

"Ye clothe you, but there is none warm" (Hag. 1:6d). The word for "clothe" in Haggai 1:6 means "to wrap around; to put on a garment or clothe (oneself or another)." To accommodate the wardrobe of the flesh, ceiled houses necessitate large closets. Men who love titles get wrapped up in higher education, paying little attention to the real Teacher (1 Jn. 2:20,27). The covering of mere men can take precedence over the headship of Christ and His Word. We have primped our lives and ministries with worldly garments. Even with all our fancy skins, we're still stark naked but don't know it. Unfortunately, man-made "aprons" only guard a religious front (Gen. 3:7). Haggai's shaking will turn Adam around! The word for "warm" in verse six comes from a primitive root which means "to be hot; figuratively, to conceive." The returning remnant had become willfully independent, each demanding his privacy (Hag. 1:9). But one cannot be "warm" alone! It takes two to "conceive," to spend quality time, to bring forth fruit (Eccles. 4:11). Meaningful relationships are discussed in Chapter Two of my book *The Issues of Life* (Shippensburg, PA: Destiny Image Publishers, 1992). Unshakeable peace conveys unbroken covenant.

2 Kings 4:34, KJV

> *And he went up, and lay upon the child, and put his mouth upon his mouth, and his eyes upon his eyes, and his hands upon his hands: and he stretched himself upon the child; and the flesh of the child waxed warm.*

Jesus wants His mouth on our mouth, His eyes on our eyes, His hands on our hands. The "warmth" of His Word and vision must come upon the Church; the signs and wonders from His hand will follow. The One with heavenly vision is stretching Himself out upon the lifeless—people, preachers, and praise—cold things (Rev. 3:15-16). Gradually warm up to the realization that without Him, we labor in vain.

"...A bag with holes"—this is literally, "a bag pierced through with holes." Misplaced priorities have hit us hard, especially in finances. God's economic *remedy* is a global seizure that shakes loose the silver and gold (Hag. 2:6-9). In Haggai's day, King Cyrus had financed the Jewish undertaking. The problem was not a lack of cash but poor stewardship and mismanaged funds. The remnant's money had disappeared like flour through a sieve. Rising prices and inflation eventually got their attention. The word for "earneth wages" in Haggai 1:6 means "to hire" and comes from a primitive root meaning "to purchase." It is translated as "buy," or "prepare" in the King James Version (Jn. 4:36; Rom. 6:23; 2 Pet. 3:15). Who are you working for? Who is your source? Is it your money or His money? Is it being used to build His house or your house? Wages are the fruit of labor, harvest's reward. Each man reaps the wages of life or death, righteousness or unrighteousness. Today, the day of the Lord, is pay day.

The word for "bag" means "a parcel (as packed up)" and comes from a root meaning "to cramp." Locally, nationally, and globally, the pressures of fiscal calamity have made things tight (Job 14:17). The word for "holes" is a primitive root meaning "to puncture, literally (to perforate, with more or less violence) or figuratively (to specify, designate, libel)." It has been translated as "bore, curse, pierce, strike through." Christians tithe and offer; thieves don't (Mal. 3:8-12; Jn. 10:1). A thief, like Judas holding the bag, tries to get into the Kingdom on his own terms. A thief is out for himself and no one else. His unjust gain will be consumed, his ways pierced through (Prov. 14:12; Zech. 5:4). God had warned His people about the shameful consequences of disobedience (Deut. 28:17-24; Jer. 12:13). A "bag with holes"—constant financial struggle—comes to those who run to their own houses. There is a better way: a purse that won't wear out, treasures in Heaven (Mt. 6:33; Lk. 12:33).

Just for Emphasis

Hag. 1:7, KJV

Thus saith the Lord of hosts; Consider your ways.

Hag. 1:7, NIV

This is what the Lord Almighty says: "Give careful thought to your ways."

Hag. 1:7, TLB

"Think it over," says the Lord of Hosts. "Consider how you have acted and what has happened as a result!"

Haggai restates his admonition (Hag. 1:5,7), revealing the divine urgency of his message and reinforcing the argument found in verse six. When God wants to emphasize something, He repeats Himself. Haggai's community was totally preoccupied with selfish pursuits. Driven to have more, they actually had less. Today, many work an extra job yet never see ends meet, their shortage correlated to their neglect of God's purpose and calling. Are you content? Are you fulfilled? Are you and your family happy or miserable? Perhaps you need to remember God's house. There is tremendous global anxiety. Accumulating natural things is not the answer.

1 Tim. 6:7-10, NIV

For we brought nothing into the world, and we can take nothing out of it.

But if we have food and clothing, we will be content with that.

People who want to get rich fall into temptation and a trap and into many foolish and harmful desires that plunge men into ruin and destruction.

For the love of money is a root of all kinds of evil. Some people, eager for money, have wandered from the faith and pierced themselves with many griefs.

Many preachers have been snared by the love of money, their appetite for success never satisfied. Some have swindled and violated the people with gimmickry and chicanery. What they raise money for is not worth supporting. Inwardly, they are unfulfilled, unclothed, naked, and ashamed. Things outside of Christ leave men empty. We will never be happy until we hear from God and do what He says. But His calling is often to ruined places. The Holy Spirit is drawn to unlikely, chaotic conditions, wrecked situations within and without (Gen. 1:2). God summons men to undesirable places and teams them with unwanted people. In the story of the Good Samaritan (Lk. 10:29-36), religion could not help broken humanity. Jesus did not come to sinful man by chance; He came by choice.

The law of love is giving (Jn. 3:16). Love your neighbor as yourself. Turn your wasted howling wilderness into the garden of Eden, and you won't want to leave it. The unattractive places of least potential may be the next Azuza Street or North Battleford. This principle jaywalks against the standard Madison Avenue approach with its feasibility studies and marketing techniques. The location with more resources and opportunities for productivity may appear to be more appealing, but every man's heart must honestly ask, "Where does God want *me*? What is His will for *my* life at this time?" Lasting satisfaction comes by being involved with that which contains God's desire and pleasure, no matter how ruined it looks. Turn your heart back to Him. Consider your ways.

Go Up to the Mountain

Hag. 1:8, KJV

Go up to the mountain, and bring wood, and build the house; and I will take pleasure in it, and I will be glorified, saith the Lord.

Hag. 1:8, NIV

"Go up into the mountains and bring down timber and build the house, so that I may take pleasure in it and be honored," says the Lord.

Hag. 1:8, TLB

"...rebuild My Temple, and I will be pleased with it and appear there in My glory," says the Lord.

Haggai 1:1-4 records Jehovah's *rebuke*. Verses 5-11 unfold His *remedy*, and verse eight is His key to it. The word for "go up" here and in Ezra 1:3 is *alah* (Strong's #5927) and means "to ascend (literally and figuratively)." *Vine's* adds that *alah* means "to go up, offer up." It is used in a variety of ways:

1. *To move from a lower to a higher place (Gen. 2:6).*

2. *To rise up or ascend (Is. 14:13).*

3. *To take a journey (Gen. 13:1)*

4. *To extend or reach (Josh. 18:12).*

5. *To go up to Palestine or Jerusalem (Ezra 2:1).*

6. *To go up to battle (Josh. 22:12).*

The "mountain" of the Lord prefigures the "heavenly places" of Ephesians 1:3 and 2:6; there, all is God's. To "go up" is to move beyond Passover and Pentecost to the Feast of Tabernacles, to extend one's borders, to enlarge one's heart for greater vision. It is to ascend the hill of the Lord, to go up to Jerusalem, to Zion (Heb. 12:22-24). To "go up" is to participate in a higher dimension of spiritual warfare (Eph. 6:12).

The verb form of *alah* is used causatively to signify "presenting an offering" to God. In 63 cases, the word is associated with the presentation of the *olah*, the whole burnt offering, the ascending offering (Lev. 1). In this foremost of the offerings, God received all. *Alah* is in the same word family as *Elyon,* meaning "the upper or the highest." *El-elyon,* or "the Most High God," is the divine name associated with the Most Holy Place and the priesthood after the order of Melchisedec (Heb. 5:1–8:6).

To "go up" to the mountain is to participate in Jesus' more excellent ministry, the royal priesthood: a family of prophets, priests, and kings (1 Pet. 2:9; Rev. 1:6). It is to worship the Most High God with the most high saints in the Most Holy Place. To go up is to press the upward calling, to sit down as an overcomer in His throne of grace, the mercy seat (Dan. 7:22; Rev. 3:21). To go up to the mountain is to become a living sacrifice, a whole burnt offering (Rom. 12:1). Jesus, the supreme Sacrifice, is our example (Eph. 5:2; Heb. 9:26; 10:12). Let us follow in His steps (Phil. 2:17; 4:18). Get God's vision for your life, then present your body to him.

Five Mountains

"Go up to the mountain…" (Hag. 1:8). The word for "mountain" is *har* (Strong's #2022) and means "a mountain or range of hills." It comes from a root that means "to loom up." The "mountain" is a symbol for the Kingdom of God, especially with regard to Mount Zion. We are to ascend into the heavenlies, the realm of the Spirit.

Five mountains now loom up before the Church. They are the essence of Haggai's *remedy*, each representing an aspect of Jesus' life and ministry. The Pattern Son walked in an open heaven, constantly led by the Spirit (Rom. 8:14). Called to be like their Lord, His Church must also experience:

1. *Mount Moriah—Kingdom sacrifice.*

2. *Mount Sinai—Kingdom obedience.*

3. *Mount Olivet—Kingdom prayer.*

4. *Mount Calvary—Kingdom compliance.*

5. *Mount Zion—Kingdom authority.*

Gen. 22:2, KJV

*And He said, Take now thy son, thine only son
Isaac, whom thou lovest, and get thee into the land of
Moriah; and offer him there for a burnt offering upon
one of the mountains which I will tell thee of.*

2 Chron. 3:1, KJV

*Then Solomon began to build the house of the Lord
at Jerusalem in mount Moriah, where the Lord appeared
unto David his father, in the place that David had
prepared in the threshingfloor of Ornan the Jebusite.*

"Moriah" means "seen of Jah, vision of Jehovah,
revelation of Jah." Mentioned in but two places, Moriah
is the mountain of Kingdom sacrifice. There Abraham
presented Isaac, typifying the Father offering up His
only Son (Jn. 3:16). Moriah was also the building site for
Solomon's Temple, chosen by David and paid for with
great sacrifice, the "full price" (1 Chron. 21:18-24).

The Church must see the Lord to receive the revelation
of His Name and character. The fear of the Lord is the beginning of all wisdom and knowledge (Prov. 1:7). Moriah is the
place where God commences to build Himself into us. From
the start of our climb, we must know that His Kingdom, like
the "full price" of Ornan's threshingfloor, will cost us everything. There is no room for cheap religion on this first mountain. We need not fear; *Jehovah-Jireh* will "see" and then
"provide" Himself for the required offering (Gen. 22:14;
Phil. 2:13). Jesus was our Ram of sacrifice.

Ex. 31:18, KJV

*And He gave unto Moses, when He had made an
end of communing with him upon mount Sinai, two*

tables of testimony, tables of stone, written with the finger of God.

Neh. 9:13, KJV

Thou camest down also upon mount Sinai, and spakest with them from heaven, and gavest them right judgments, and true laws, good statutes and commandments.

The second mountain is "Sinai" and means "cliff, deep ravine, precipitous, sharp, jagged." It is mentioned most frequently in the Pentateuch with regard to the ministry of Moses, the mediator of the law. Sinai is the mountain of Kingdom obedience. There the finger of God imparted the law, the Decalogue, the Ten Commandments.

Once committed to be a living sacrifice, the Church must scale the dangerous heights of Sinai. There the law of God is written on the fleshly tables of our hearts (2 Cor. 3:1-3). The deep ravines of legalism and license are all about, but the royal law of Christ's life is a perfect compass (Jas. 1:25; 2:8,12). The One who fulfilled all righteousness was perfectly obedient, the unbroken tables of the Law.

2 Sam. 15:30, KJV

And David went up by the ascent of mount Olivet, and wept as he went up, and had his head covered, and he went barefoot: and all the people that was with him covered every man his head, and they went up, weeping as they went up.

Lk. 21:37, KJV

And in the day time He was teaching in the temple;
and at night He went out, and abode in the mount that
is called the mount of Olives.

"Olivet" is the third mountain and means "an olive
(as yielding illuminating oil), the tree, the branch, or the
berry." It comes from the root *Ziv* (Strong's #2099) which
means "to be prominent; brightness; Zif, the month of
flowers (corresponding to May)." The Greek word is
similar, adding "an olive orchard, garden or grove; a
place set with olive trees; Mount of Olives." Olivet is the
mountain of Kingdom prayer. There in imperial solitude
the ancient monarch found refuge from Absalom.
David's greater Son found this quiet garden to be a personal haven from evil men and hateful Pharisees.

Our upward calling to become a living sacrifice requires
walking in obedience. The secret to scaling the path of
life is the prominent practice of intercessory prayer, else
we may faint in our ascent (Prov. 4:18; Lk. 18:1). Gethsemane means "olive press." Prayer brings illumination
and spiritual understanding. Olivet is the ascent of tears;
we will weep as we go up. As with Moses in his walk,
the priest in his worship, and Joshua in his warfare, men
ascend Olivet barefooted. There we learn to groan with
our great High Priest in the life of intercession.

Lk. 23:33, KJV

And when they were come to the place, which is
called Calvary, there they crucified Him, and the

malefactors, one on the right hand, and the other on the left.

Jn. 19:17, KJV

And He bearing His cross went forth into a place called the place of a skull, which is called in the Hebrew Golgotha.

The fourth mountain is "Calvary"; the Greek word is *kranion* (Strong's #2898) which means "a skull (cranium)." *Vine's* adds, "a head." It is a derivative of the base of *kar* which means "the hair of the head; a horn." The Hebrew root for "Golgotha" means "round (shaped like a head); a head (as enumeration of persons)," and it comes from a root that means "to roll." It is rendered as "every man" with regard to the manna and the shekel of the sanctuary (Ex. 16:16; 38:26). Calvary is the mountain of complete Kingdom compliance—full surrender to do the Father's will. There Jesus Christ, the Horn of our salvation, the Head of the Church, was crucified. In that awful place, all men were polled and found wanting; Jesus tasted death for every man; and sin was rolled away (Jn. 1:29). He is the Bread that came down from heaven, atonement's price for every man.

Sacrifice, obedience, and prayer bring us to the foot of the cross, the point of denial and death of self. Going forth unto Him outside the camp, bearing His reproach, we discover the grace to forgive all men, to commit our spirits into the hand of the Father (Heb. 13:10-13). We fully comply, completely surrender to carry out the delight and pleasure of our Shearer (Jn. 8:29; Acts 8:32-33).

On Olivet we take the bitter cup and give thanks...on Calvary, we drink it.

2 Sam. 5:7, KJV

Nevertheless David took the strong hold of Zion: the same is the city of David.

Heb. 12:22, NIV

But you have come to Mount Zion, to the heavenly Jerusalem, the city of the living God. You have come to thousands upon thousands of angels in joyful assembly,

to the church of the firstborn, whose names are written in heaven....

Finally, we crest the summit. The fifth mountain is "Zion" which means "sunny, very dry, clear, unobstructed, set up, placed, established, fortress, monument, landmark." It is mentioned mostly in Book of Psalms (38 times), Isaiah (47 times), Jeremiah (17 times), and Lamentations (15 times). Zion is the mountain of Kingdom authority. Both testaments present the two dominant themes that are associated with Zion: the king and the priest. Zion was the ruling city of King David, the capital city, the governing city of the nation. Zion was also the city of the Tabernacle of David, the sacred city. David ruled in Zion; the government of God was revealed in the kingdom of David. In Zion, its shepherd-king led the nation in ordered worship under a simple, single tent. In the New Testament, Zion (in a general sense) is the Church, and (more specificly), it designates the overcomers within the Church, those apprehended for the high calling, destined to rule and reign with Him from the mercy seat within the veil.

Moriah, Sinai, Olivet, Calvary...all these predicate Mount Zion, catching us up to the throne of God (Rev. 12:5). The triumphant Church who identifies with the fellowship of His sufferings will know Him in the power of His resurrection and exaltation. Jesus Christ has been given all executive authority, Haggai's signet ring. Mature sons, those He unashamedly calls brethren, will prevail and govern with Him (Rom. 8:29). The distressed men who shared David's humiliation and hardship in the dark loneliness of Adullam later reigned as mighty men, administering the authority of his kingdom from the hill of the Lord.

Sacrifice, obedience, prayer, compliance, authority...all qualities of Jesus' life and ministry. May we daily bear in our body these marks of the Lord, His divine nature tabernacled and manifested through holy flesh (Gal. 6:17; Rev. 3:21). Let Christ be magnified.

Bring Wood

Go up, ascend, awake, arise. The required materials to rebuild His house cannot be found in this present dimension. Everything we need is over our heads, above our feverish entanglement with lesser things (Eph. 1:3; Col. 3:1-3).

The word for "wood" in Haggai 1:8 means "tree, wood, timber, stick, stalk." Wood symbolizes *humanity*. Most of the furniture in Moses' tabernacle was made of acacia wood, then overlayed with brass or gold. Solomon's temple contained cedar and fir (cypress).

Cyrus' grant had released funds to buy timber for Zerubbabel's temple (Ezra 3:7; 6:4). When a man ascends the hill of the Lord, he carries his own humanity, working out his own salvation with fear and trembling. The Lord lays the ax to the root of our being on the top of the mountain (Mt. 3:10). This bloody scene of sacrifice is the place of great exchange: our wood for His. Men tend to build their own houses with scraps of wood, hay, and stubble, efforts of self to produce the nature of God. Mere human wisdom and strength can never receive His pleasure or contain His glory. Our intellect, emotions, and will must be lugged to the top of Moriah, then burned with fire. Those living outside His rest are not committed to His will. Much of what we are doing is being built for our own needs and desires, not God's.

Go up to the mountain and bring wood—your wood to exchange for His, your humanity for His, your flesh for His—our life for His life (Gal. 2:20). Jesus' humanity is new timber, "holy flesh" (Jer. 11:15, Hag. 2:12)! This holy flesh is the sinless life He lived as the consecrated habitation of the Father—the holy life of sacrifice, obedience, prayer, compliance, and authority (Heb. 4:15). The corporate temple must be built in His image and finished with the same essentials (2 Cor. 3:18). Jesus Christ is the consecrated Ram who sanctified the royal priesthood; His life was offered once and for all that we might live (Ex. 29:34; Heb. 10:10). The Pauline epistles unfold the mystery of godliness, His Incarnation (1 Tim. 3:16). At the end of Chapter Seven of my book, *Rest in the Day of Trouble*, (Shippensburg, PA: Destiny Image Publishers, 1993) is a list of references showing Jesus Christ to be God Almighty manifested in the flesh (as in Lk. 24:39; Jn. 1:14; Rom. 8:3; Heb. 2:14; 4:15).

Rom. 6:6-7, NIV

For we know that our old self was crucified with Him so that the body of sin might be done away with, that we should no longer be slaves to sin—

because anyone who has died has been freed from sin.

The mystery of godliness is basic yet profound. Simply stated, the "body of sin" we lived in before conversion was unholy flesh; now that we have been born from above, our bodies have become the temple or house of God the Holy Spirit, our members weapons and instruments of His righteousness (Rom. 6:19). We go up the mountain with our old life and return with new timber: His new life—a new heart, a new mind, a new tongue.

2 Tim. 1:9-11, NIV

Who has saved us and called us to a holy life—not because of anything we have done but because of his own purpose and grace. This grace was given us in Christ Jesus before the beginning of time,

but it has now been revealed through the appearing of our Savior, Christ Jesus, who has destroyed death and has brought life and immortality to light through the gospel.

And of this gospel I was appointed a herald and an apostle and a teacher.

In a much deeper sense, Haggai 1:8 plumbs the mystery of the light of life (Jn. 8:12), the understanding of resurrection life and immortality. The chart below will begin to explain the scope of this revelation.

Our Wood	His Wood
Our old humanity	His new humanity
Our unholy flesh	His holy flesh
The body of sin (Rom. 6:6)	The body of Christ
The body of death (Rom. 7:24)	The body of life
The body of darkness (Lk. 11:34)	The body of light
Terrestrial body (1 Cor. 15:40)	Celestial body
A natural body (1 Cor. 15:44)	A spiritual body
Our vile body (Phil. 3:21)	His glorious body

Col. 2:9, KJV

For in him dwelleth all the fulness of the Godhead bodily.

Col. 2:9, NIV

For in Christ all the fullness of the Deity lives in bodily form.

Herein lies His ultimate intention: God pours all of Himself into a body; He finishes the temple, and He fills it with His glory! Some aspects of this truth are yet veiled, part of a full salvation ready to be revealed (Eph. 5:23; 1 Thess. 5:23; 1 Pet. 1:5). This shall take place when the "Desire of all nations" shall come (Hag. 2:7).

2 Cor. 5:1-5, KJV

For we know that if our earthly house of this taber-nacle were dissolved, we have a building of God, an house not made with hands, eternal in the heavens.

For in this we groan, earnestly desiring to be clothed upon with our house which is from heaven:

If so be that being clothed we shall not be found naked.

For we that are in this tabernacle do groan, being burdened: not for that we would be unclothed, but clothed upon, that mortality might be swallowed up of life.

Now He that hath wrought us for the selfsame thing is God, who also hath given unto us the earnest of the Spirit.

2 Cor. 5:5, NIV

Now it is God who has made us for this very purpose and has given us the Spirit as a deposit, guaranteeing what is to come.

Our body is the temple of the Holy Spirit, and we have died to the law by the body of Christ (Rom. 7:24-25). The restored Church built by the heavenly Zerubbabel is to be fashioned with new beams (Mt. 16:18). The ascended life is not to be found *down here*; it is hidden in Christ at the top of the mountain (Col. 3:1-3). We are members of His flesh and of His bones (Eph. 5:30). Both Pauline and Johannine theology unfold the fellowship of this mystery, the communion of the Body of Christ (1 Cor. 10:16; 1 Jn. 1:1-5). Men rich in understanding, like Joseph of Arimethaea, crave and beg for the body of Jesus (Mk. 15:43; Lk. 23:52). The Church is to be presented in holiness, having been circumcised and sanctified (Col. 1:22; 2:11; Heb. 13:12). Moses and the elders ascended the mountain and saw the glorious

Church, "the body of heaven in His clearness"—the Body of Christ—fashioned and conformed to His image and nature (Ex. 24:10). The earth is His footstool, and all this is "under His feet."

Though lofty, these truths remain pragmatic. Consider the holy flesh, the Spirit-temple of the two men who helped shape the historical Book of Acts: Peter and Paul. These apostles to the circumcision (Peter, Acts 1–12) and the uncircumcision (Paul, Acts 13–28) manifested the resurrection life of Jesus Christ in their mortal bodies (Acts 5:15; 19:12; Rom. 8:11).

Go up to the mountain and bring down His life; the Tree of life is Jesus Christ, the One who *is* the resurrection (Jn. 11:25)! The first man Adam was a living soul; the last Adam is a quickening or life-giving spirit (1 Cor. 15:44-49). The life of the first Adam comes from the tree of the knowledge of good and evil. The resurrection life of Jesus Christ comes from the tree of life (Gen. 2:9; 3:22-24). See also Proverbs 3:18; 11:30; 13:12; 15:4 and Revelation 2:7; 22:2,14. The resurrection is a Person!

Go up to the mountain and bring wood—His new humanity, His holy flesh. Climb Jacob's ladder (Gen. 28:12). Ascend the hill of the Lord. Become a partaker of the divine nature. Let heaven come down to earth, let His House be built, let His will be done (Mt. 6:10; Rev. 21:1-11).

For His Pleasure

"…and I will take pleasure in it…" (Hag. 1:8). The Father is building the house that will embody and then disperse His glory to the nations. Jesus was the Son in whom the Father was well pleased. The Church, the corporate house, must be built with the same quality of life that Christ lived among men, formed into the "same image" (2 Cor. 3:18; Col. 1:15).

The word for "pleasure" in Haggai 1:8 means "to be pleased with; specifically, to satisfy a debt; to accept favorably." It is translated in the King James Version many ways, including "approve, delight, enjoy, favor." Solomon's temple received an anointing of glory (1 Kings 9:3; 2 Chron. 7:16). The greater one was the temple that housed the Father (Mt. 12:42, Jn. 1:14). At His baptism and on the Mount of Transfiguration, the Father was glorified in the Son (Mt. 3:16-17; 17:5). Once the Church is well-pleasing to the Father, the nations will hear us (Jn. 8:29).

The literal Hebrew of Haggai 1:8 reads, "I will get glory to Myself," or "I will glorify Myself." The word for "glorified" is *kabad* (Strong's #3513), a primitive root meaning "to be heavy...in a good sense (numerous, rich, honorable)." *Vine's* adds that *kabad* means "to honor." Compare Haggai 2:3 and 9 for the full etymology of this word. The Feast of Ingathering is upon us. The Grecian inquiry, the cry of the nations, is the signal for the Son of Man to be glorified (Jn. 12:20-23). The Father glorified His nature in Jesus, the Pattern Son; He will glorify it again in a people for His name (see Jn. 13:31; 14:13; 15:8; Acts 15:14; 2 Thess. 1:12). Eschatologically, not one verse in the Bible says that Jesus will come "for" the saints. Before He comes "with" the saints from Heaven, He will be glorified "in" the saints on earth (see Jn. 17:10; Rom. 8:17,30; 1 Thess. 4:14; 2 Thess. 1:10).

The Father who exalted and honored Jesus is bringing many sons to the same measure of glory (Eph. 4:13; Heb. 2:10). The prophet's *rebuke* was followed by the divine *remedy*: go up to the mountain and bring wood, then build a house for God's pleasure and glory.

Too Busy for God

Hag. 1:9, KJV

Ye looked for much, and, lo, it came to little; and when ye brought it home, I did blow upon it. Why? saith the Lord of hosts. Because of Mine house that is waste, and ye run every man unto his own house.

Hag. 1:9, NIV

...while each of you is busy with his own house.

Hag. 1:9, TLB

You hope for much but get so little. And when you bring it home, I blow it away—it doesn't last at all. Why? Because My Temple lies in ruins, and you don't care. Your only concern is your own fine homes.

After soaring through the heavenlies in verse eight, the prophet brings us back to earth in verse nine. There was a direct connection between the remnant's poverty and their neglect of the temple (Hos. 2:8). This Hebrew infinitive literally reads, "a looking for much," and describes the remnant's constant, repeated anticipation of plenty. The word for "looked" in verse nine means "to turn; to face, appear, look." Men have their own expectations or brazenly interpret God's (Lk. 24:21). In Haggai

1:6, the remnant sowed "much" and brought in "little"; here they looked for "much" and it came to "little." Part of the answer lies in the expression "lo"—an indication of surprise that reveals the callous estate of Haggai's community.

Is. 17:10-11, NIV

> *You have forgotten God your Savior; you have not remembered the Rock, your fortress. Therefore, though you set out the finest plants and plant imported vines,*
>
> *though on the day you set them out, you make them grow, and on the morning when you plant them, you bring them to bud, yet the harvest will be as nothing in the day of disease and incurable pain.*

The word for "home" in Haggai 1:9 is the same for "house" in verse two—the environment of the self-indulgent. The singular house of the Lord took second place to their "home" life, their ceiled houses. To "blow" means "to puff; literally, blow hard, scatter, kindle, expire; figuratively, to disesteem." The crop vanished; God "blew it away." The little that was harvested was scattered by Jehovah (2 Sam. 22:16; Is. 54:16). This temporal realm of grassy flesh is being consumed by the breath of eternal Spirit (Is. 40:7).

The interrogative "why" echoes the hard-hearted ignorance of the priesthood related in the Book of Malachi. Men shadowbox demons when it is the Lord with whom they must contend. He, not the devil, is mercifully shutting down ministries all over the land. Denominational agendas and plans that dishonor the Lord's purpose are feeling His blast of discipline (Ps. 39:11; Hag. 2:17).

The word for "waste" (Hag. 1:4) is described by the apostle Paul in terms of spiritual reality of atrophy and eventual collapse.

1 Cor. 11:30, KJV

For this cause many are weak and sickly among you, and many sleep.

Haggai continues in verse nine to show the remnant their pre-occupation with themselves and the widespread neglect of corporate vision: "...and ye run every man unto his own house" (Hag. 1:9). This is literally, "You are running..." Knox's translation says, "You run helter-skelter." This word means "to run quickly" or "to rush," picturing the zeal with which the remnant pursued their own affairs. The word "unto" means "with reference to, in the interest of." We are a mobile society in a mad rush to go nowhere. Busy, busy, busy...with our own house, or what we think His house is. We are zealous, but do we know Him? (Rom. 10:1-3.) Don't run to your house in vain (Ps. 119:132). A similar Greek word is *suntrecho* which means "to rush together (hastily assemble) or headlong" (Acts 1:18; 1 Pet. 4:4; Job 5:13). We are running head-first, not heart-first (1 Cor. 9:24; Gal. 5:7).

The word for "man" in Haggai 1:9 is *ish* and means "a nobleman, or a man of high degree." It targets the new creation man—our noble calling in Christ. This *ish* man has the mind of humility and service exemplified by Jesus, Paul, Timothy, and Epaphroditus (Phil. 2:4,21). Contrast this against those flamboyant leaders who build pillars in their "own name" (2 Sam. 18:18). Jesus went to Mt. Olivet while every man went to his own house (Jn. 7:53; 8:1).

1 Kings 7:1, KJV

But Solomon was building his own house thirteen years...

1 Kings 6:37-38, KJV

In the fourth year was the foundation of the house of the Lord laid...

And in the eleventh year...was the house finished.... So he was seven years in building it.

No More Dew

Hag. 1:10, KJV

Therefore the heaven over you is stayed from dew and the earth is stayed from her fruit.

Hag. 1:10, NIV

Therefore, because of you the heavens have withheld their dew and the earth its crops.

Hag. 1:10, TLB

That is why I am holding back the rains from heaven and giving you such scant crops.

Hag. 1:10, Knox

That is why the skies are forbidden to rain on you, earth to afford its bounty.

Dew was important to the harvest, especially in August and September, to prevent ripening grain from wilting in the heat. By the simple expedient of withholding rain or dew, God reduced human pride and self-sufficiency.

This literally reads, "Therefore, for you" or "on account of you" or "for your sakes..." The word for "therefore" means "set upright; just; rightly or so," showing just judgment. Shall not the Judge of all the earth do right? The *heaven* represents the realm of the Spirit; God shut the heavenlies. The word for "stayed" in verse 10 means "to restrict, by act (hold back or in) or word (prohibit)." The word for "dew" comes from a primitive root which means "to strew over; by implication, to cover in or plate (with beams)." God wanted His House covered with dew, not their cedar.

Dew can symbolize the Word of God or the Holy Spirit. *Jehovah-Tsebaoth* had closed the heavens, removing His favor and blessing (Ps. 133:3; Prov. 19:12). Religion is the attempt of men and demons to replace the doctrine of Christ with impressive substitutes (Deut. 32:2). In most places, there is little unity or real intercession, just wall-to-wall menpleasers (Song 5:2; Hos. 14:5).

Mic. 5:7, NIV

The remnant of Jacob will be in the midst of many peoples like dew from the Lord, like showers on the grass, which do not wait for man or linger for mankind.

The word for "earth" in Haggai 1:10 means "to be firm" and is rendered as "country, earth, field, ground, land, world" in the King James Version. The word for "fruit" means "produce; a crop; figuratively, wealth; increase," and comes from a root meaning "to flow, to bring with pomp." The *earth* is the soil of men's hearts; the *fruit*, His divine nature (Mt. 13:18; 21:43; Gal. 5:22-23).

Without the dew of His Word and Spirit, there can be no fruitful increase. Men have built paneled houses void of the divine flow and genuine pomp of pure worship (Jn. 4:23-24).

God's Drought

Hag. 1:11, KJV

And I called for a drought upon the land, and upon the mountains, and upon the corn, and upon the new wine, and upon the oil, and upon that which the ground bringeth forth, and upon men, and upon cattle, and upon all the labour of the hands.

Hag. 1:11, NIV

I called for a drought on the fields...and whatever the ground produces....

Hag. 1:11, TLB

In fact, I have called for a drought upon the land, yes, and in the highlands too; a drought to wither the grain and grapes and olives and all your other crops, a drought to starve both you and all your cattle and ruin everything you have worked so hard to get.

The Lord's chastisement adjusts our lives back to His primary purpose. While busily erecting irrelevant things, we have been reluctant to face the unfinished condition of God's house. We have hidden ourselves in distractions and secondary goals in spite of reaping little from brash expectations. This drought from the Lord affected nine areas, the biblical number of finality. It touched everything. Nothing was exempted. Through this experience,

Jehovah brought a lasting end to the remnant's desire to build their own private lives. The prophetic *rebuke* led to the divine *remedy*. The cure would produce the resolve to hear the real Word of the Lord. The dearth that restored a communal thirst for God impacted the remnant's whole world:

1. *The land.*

2. *The mountains.*

3. *The corn.*

4. *The new wine.*

5. *The oil.*

6. *The fruit of the ground.*

7. *The men.*

8. *The cattle.*

9. *The labor of the hands.*

The word for "called" in Haggai 1:11 means "to call out to, to address by name; to accost a person met." This word means to name something, and specifies sovereignty over it. God, not man, is in charge. The word for "drought" means "drought or desolation." The womb of the morning has been made barren by the Lord Himself. Having come to the birth, we have only produced the wind of doctrine (Is. 26:18; Eph. 4:14). But the desolate one is about to bear many sons; the forsaken cities are about to be inhabited (Is. 54:1).

The word for "land" in verse eleven is the same as "earth" in verse ten, and represents the hearts of men. Jesus talked about four kinds of soil, the condition of the inner man (Mt. 13:18-23). Idolatrous hearts, though dry and hard (Jer. 50:38), will turn at the hearing of His Word.

God's drought touched the mountains; the forests suffered. The word for "mountains" is the same as verse eight and can represent all the kingdoms of men (Hag. 2:22). In the day when His Church is perfected, every tree will bow its knee to the earth's rightful King (Rev. 11:15).

Jehovah proceeded to dry up the corn, wine, and oil, the chief products of Palestine. The word for "corn" means "increase; grain." Its root is translated as the word "grow" in the King James Version. The corn, the Word of God, makes men grow. The grain has withered (Joel 1:17), yet we have not cried unto the Lord (Hos. 7:14). But the overcoming Church will become a handful of corn in the top of the mountain; the Lord has opened the heavens and restored His Word (Ps. 4:7; 65:13; 72:16; 78:24).

Ps. 65:9, NIV

You care for the land and water it; you enrich it abundantly. The streams of God are filled with water to provide the people with grain, for so you have ordained it.

The word for "new wine" in verse 11 means "fresh grape-juice (as just squeezed out)." As previously noted, wine emphasizes the joy of the Holy Spirit (Ps. 16:11), and it is part of our offering unto the Lord (Neh. 10:39; 13:12). Running to one's own house brings sorrow and sighing; the new wine is found only in the cluster of corporate vision (Is. 24:7; 65:8). Naive Christians get drunk on sad, unscriptural songs that extol the flesh and worship the devil, then err and stumble in judgment (Hos. 9:2; Joel 1:5). But He has preserved new wine for a new bottle (Lk. 5:37-38). Let the heathen rage; the goodness of the Lord is being poured from His presence (Prov. 3:10; Zech. 9:17; Acts 2:13).

Joel 3:18, KJV

And it shall come to pass in that day, that the mountains shall drop down new wine....

The word for "oil" in Haggai 1:11 means "oil (as producing light); figuratively, anointing"—a powerful emblem for the Holy Spirit. Darkness is ignorance: Light is understanding (Eph. 1:18). Many have languished, some even been destroyed (Joel 1:10; Hos. 4:6). But the Lord is bringing a fresh anointing upon sons of oil who willingly welcome His remedy (Num. 11:8; Zech. 4:14).

Ps. 92:10, KJV

...I shall be anointed with fresh oil.

What a drought! The land, the mountains, the corn, the oil, and the wine...all smashed by the hand of the Lord. But there is more. The fruit of the ground, men, cattle, and all their labor would also wither away at His stroke. Jehovah burned up their national product. The word for "ground" in Haggai 1:11 means "soil (from its general redness)" and comes from the root word *adam*. The word for "bringeth forth" means "to come forth, go out, proceed, go forth, bring out." When Adam runs to his own house, he forsakes the merciful God who alone can bring him out of bondage (Hag. 2:5). This truth is accentuated in verse eleven—the word for "men" is *adam*. Adam is drying up...Adam is dying. God killed him at the cross (Rom. 6:6).

The word for "cattle" is collective, and it refers to any large quadruped or animal. In the Old Testament, riches were often measured in flocks and herds. God's drought encompasses our possessions; the word for "all" in this verse means "the whole; hence, all, any, or every (often in a plural sense)." The famine disannulled all labor expended in cultivation. This word in verse 11 means "toil; hence, a work, produce, property (as the result of labor)." God had warned that the locust and strangers would eat their labor (Ps. 78:46; 109:11). The remnant Church strove for that which did not gratify (Is. 55:2; Jer. 3:24; 20:5).

Prisoners of Expectation

Zech. 9:12, KJV

Turn you to the strong hold, ye prisoners of hope....

The private goal of the remnant was to build a striking, formidable house of their own, so God blew on it (Hag. 1:9), drying up everything they had built for themselves in His name. Christ in us is the hope of glory (Col. 1:27). We are prisoners of that expectation, but we habitually put our own interpretation on the divine anticipation! In our lust for success, we attach the name of the Lord to our own plans, rationalizing these self-efforts by "giving Him the glory." But amidst all our personal pursuits and "noble" humanism, the temple of God still lies unfinished.

The climate of man-made zeal is marked by much busyness (Rom. 10:2). Most ministries necessarily vacillate from one spiritual fad to another. Every year the emphasis changes, with little or no continuity in the pursued vision. Preachers, desperate for results, take on the world's mentality: the end justifies the means. But God is neither interested nor impressed by our paltry crop. He just keeps on blowing down everything He did not tell us to do. Our slavish preoccupation for crunching numbers must be replaced with a greater spiritual attraction—a renewed involvement with the waste places, the house of the Lord. We must be delivered from the passing to the permanent. Meaningful living moves forward in what God has foreordained. It may be difficult to make this shift, but if what we're doing gets dry enough, we'll change!

There is widespread disappointment among the people of God; things have not worked out as anticipated. With all the hype, there is not much happening. But our heavenly Father is using this sense of failure to turn us. The divine drought comes to liberate His people from strategies and enterprises that have not reproduced His name in the earth. The strength of man permeates our activities, and that spells trouble. Whether in the form of covert motivation or high-energy method, every human promotion, even when "done for the Lord," is doomed to fail.

Lk. 24:21,27, NIV

But we had hoped that He was the one who was going to redeem Israel...

*And beginning with Moses and all the Prophets, He
explained to them what was said in all the Scriptures
concerning Himself.*

Cleophas and his young friend had their own interpretation of the Messianic expectation. Their theology
and eschatology demanded a Deliverer that accom-
modated the Judaistic agenda. Jesus ignored their whin-
ing, and He began to expound or interpret Himself
throughout the Old Testament! His impartation opened
their eyes to divine perspective. Men stubbornly refuse
to give up their favorite toys until God empties their
playpens. Failure can be a good thing if it turns a man
back to the right direction. Has your present sphere of
involvement produced a famine in your life? Is it dry
where you live? Do you need rain?

Disillusion and frustration will save us for God's
highest purpose: the raising up of His House. Those with
the greatest potential for the high calling are men who
have suffered the greatest defeats. A true sign that one
has been apprehended for the top of the mountain (Hag.
1:8) is that the wind of God has caused his prospects and
intentions to miscarry. But what about all our teaching,
prophesying, and writing about the Feast of Tabernacles?
What about the global harvest? Aren't the nations to
come to God? Yes, but the threshing instrument for that
day will first identify with the divine Worm in humiliation and crucifixion (Ps. 22:6; Is. 41:14-15)). The way of the
cross leads to failure, then fame. Before honor is humility.

In my book, *The Hour is Come*, a study of John 12:20-33,
the question is asked, "How low will you go?" God's

heart is not afraid to get close to dying humanity. Burnt stones are men whose personal agendas have burned themselves out and everybody else around them. Weary and worn, these dimly burning wicks are unhappy with themselves and others (Mt. 12:20). Acknowledging this wasted status of God's House may not seem like the key or *remedy* to real vision. Hyper-faith extremists only measure health and wealth, the silver and gold of Haggai 2:8, with natural things. The emphasis has been upon what we "do" for God.

Since the 1980s, many great ministries have fallen into disgrace. In the few short years Russia and Eastern Europe have been available to the gospel, the fire of human zeal has begun to burn them over. With all the ballyhoo, there is little being permanently built for God in those nations. Many people have been saved, but the purpose for His corporate house still lies waste. (Will we make the same mistakes in China?) The real revival, a genuine Feast of Ingathering, is yet before us! Times of refreshing will come from the presence of the Lord to complete His temple and fill it with glory. From *that* house, *Jehovah-Tsebaoth* will jolt all nations! He will reach the whole world through the global shaking that comes out of the place of unshakeable peace and unbreakable relationships!

Called to Reconnection

God had dealt severely with His firstfruits remnant. Our Husband and Head now invites us to the top of the mountain, the place of sacrifice and transformation (Song 2:10; 4:8). There we can reconnect to God's fundamental purpose and calling. Our present vexation (His

"drought") has generated a fresh desire
rid of peripheral things, to sever ourselv
essential, inferior undertakings. The high calling has become the low calling to the ruined condition of His
people.

Will you become reinvolved with a devastated
Church? There's not a whole lot of popularity or money
in addressing the contemporary disorder throughout His
Body. Much of what is being currently staged is not
leveled at the main issue. The real house is in ruins, but
we're still not paying attention. Get reconnected. Go up
to the mountain and bring wood. Present your body and
go back to work. Give God something He can bless.

The way we are living has not brought rest. Dedicated
to temporal things that drain our momentum and ener-
gy, we have little left for the House of the Lord. Our attempts to make this present dimension more than it is
still fail to justify its emptiness. Our "houses" are worth-
less ventures; we have not produced the genuine house
of the Lord. True pleasure and fulfillment by the Spirit
lies yonder, buried in the debris and wreckage. Go
dig it out.

We have His promise of greater glory and unshakeable peace! Respond to the Lord's dream. Believe Him to
resurrect the heavenly vision of the Glorious Church. As
with Zerubbabel, Joshua, and the remnant, let Him reac-
tivate His will in your spirit (Hag. 1:14). It's easier to ig-
nore the truth and stay at a distance, concealed behind
custom-designed walls. It requires little effort to hide at
home, avoiding sacrifice and inconvenience at all costs.

Through Haggai's message, the people of Judah had been brought to its knees. The prophet's *rebuke* had instigated the divine *remedy*. The remnant was to ascend the mountain, bring fresh timber and build His House. All that remained was their *resolve* to hear the true Word of *Jehovah-Tsebaoth*!

What is the Word of the Lord? What is He saying? Where is the real voice of the Lord? Who is speaking it?

Haggai's congregation was finally ready to hear.

Chapter Four

The Resolve

"...and they came and did work..."

Haggai 1:12-15

What amazing results! In just twenty-three days, the Word of the Lord had brought the cure for discouragement. Fifteen years of unbelief and procrastination had been swallowed up in less than a month (Joel 2:25). Of all the prophets, Haggai was perhaps the most powerful in the immediate effect of his message upon his local and national situation. Receiving Jehovah's *rebuke* (Hag. 1:1-4) and knowing His *remedy* (Hag. 1:5-11) is not enough. We must be doers, not just hearers. We must *resolve* in our hearts to let His engrafted Word save us, and choose to change. The dry season had produced a fresh response to Jehovah's voice. With readiness of mind and spirit, the remnant received God's real purpose and true messenger. Haggai's ministry had made a tremendous impact, yet he took none of the credit. It was the Lord's doing.

Hag. 1:12, KJV

Then Zerubbabel the son of Shealtiel, and Joshua the son of Josedech, the high priest, with all the remnant of the people, obeyed the voice of the Lord their God, and the words of Haggai the prophet, as the Lord their God had sent him, and the people did fear before the Lord.

Hag. 1:12, TLB

...and the few people remaining in the land obeyed Haggai's message from the Lord their God; they began to worship him in earnest.

Hag. 1:12, AMP

...listened to and obeyed the voice of the Lord their God [not vaguely or partly, but completely, according to] the words of Haggai....

Zerubbabel the governor and Joshua the priest led the way in repentance and obedience. Leaders must be first partakers of harvest (Josh. 3:3,15; 2 Tim. 2:6). Spirit-filled innovators—apostles in the Body of Christ, pastors in the local church, and parents in the home—are predestined forerunners and models for this day of restoration. Once the fathers hearts are fixed, they will turn to the sons (Mal. 4:5-6). Then a "remnant" Church can respond to apostolic vision. This word means "a remainder or residual (surviving, final) portion" and is translated as "residue" in Haggai 2:3. God's people are scattered throughout the nations and denominations. The outcasts of Israel are returning to Zion (Is. 10:21; Jer. 23:3; Mic. 2:12; 4:7). The "remnant" theme is especially characteristic of Isaiah's prophecy (Is. 6:11-13; 7:3; 11:11). The name of his son Shearjashub means, "a remnant shall return." Haggai and Zechariah recognized in the small group of repatriated Jews the fulfillment of Isaiah's prophecy.

For the first time in years, the people had one mind and judgment (1 Cor. 1:10). The elders agreed with the voice of the Lord and the sheep followed their shepherds (Amos 3:3; Heb. 13:7,17). All "obeyed." This word means to "hear intelligently (often with the implication of attention and obedience)." It is translated as different words in the King James Version, i.e. "consider, discern, give ear, listen, obey, perceive, regard, understand." The whole remnant, the whole Body obeyed:

1. *The voice of the Lord their God.*

2. *The words of Haggai the prophet.*

To obey the Lord is to obey those whom He sends in His name. The word for "sent" in Haggai 1:12 is *apostello* in the Septuagint (LXX), the Greek Old Testament. The Church is presently experiencing the renaissance of apostolic ministry; God is restoring our judges as at the first (Is. 1:26). *Apostello* means "to send with full authorization." Apostles are God's authority; we are being restored back to Eden through patriarchs, or fathers (Joel 2:3; 1 Cor. 4:15). Haggai was on a foundational mission from the Lord. His mandate is also most relevant to this era when Jesus, the Chief Apostle, is building His Church (Acts 5:11-12; Heb. 3:1).

A "fear" of further calamity from Jehovah's powerful hand came upon Haggai's audience. This word in verse twelve means "to revere or stand in awe." The Bible attests this usage approximately 330 times and in reference to all periods. Their fear was not the complete evidence of a penitential state of mind (Hag. 2:10-14), but Haggai's word brought an immediate effect of unity in obedience. The "fear" of the Lord is...

1. *Clean (Ps. 19:9).*

2. *The beginning of wisdom (Ps. 111:10).*

3. *The beginning of knowledge (Prov. 1:7; 9:10).*

4. *To hate evil (Prov. 8:13).*

5. *The instruction of wisdom (Prov. 15:33).*

6. *The key to life (Prov. 10:27; 19:23; 22:4).*

7. *His treasure (Is. 33:6).*

Those truly alive in Christ are marked by this attitude of heart. The fear of the Lord is one facet of the sevenfold Messianic anointing that is flowing down from the Head onto His Body (Ps. 133; Is. 11:1-3). The word of His prophets restores godly fear to the remnant Church (1 Sam. 12:18).

In the Message

Hag. 1:13, KJV

Then spake Haggai the Lord's messenger in the Lord's message unto the people, saying, I am with you, saith the Lord.

Hag. 1:13, TLB

Then the Lord told them (again sending the message through Haggai, His messenger), "I am with you; I will bless you."

The word for "messenger" and "message" in this verse is *mal'ak* (Strong's #4397) and means "to dispatch as a deputy; a messenger; specifically, of God, an angel (also a prophet, priest, or teacher)." The King James Version translates this as "ambassador, angel, king, messenger." The name Malachi, literally, "my messenger," is based on this noun. In the Septuagint (LXX), this word is *aggelos* or "messenger, angel."

There are two great lessons here. First, one can be the Lord's messenger without being "in the Lord's message." There are many men genuinely sent from the Lord, but they are not saying anything. Second, one can parrot the Lord's message without being "the Lord's messenger." There is an element of "wild kingdom" in the Body of Christ, those with the right semantics but the wrong spirit. To illustrate this, there are both "wineskin" churches and "wine" churches. The former has good structure and sound government but is woefully lacking in understanding and proclaiming present truth. The latter has a grasp of what God is saying through apostles and prophets, but has nothing domestically or ecclesiastically to put it in.

There are many "voices" going forth in the name of prophecy, the Word of the Lord (1 Cor. 14:10) But nothing moves in the heavenlies or manifests in the earth until there arises "the Lord's messenger"—a man truly sent from God. When such ambassadors are walking "in the Lord's message," they are speaking the truth in love, agreeing with the Scriptures and reproducing the fruit of the Spirit. A renewed prophetic inspiration, a fresh spiritual sensitivity to *who* and *what* contains the undeniable voice of the Lord, is stirring us back to our one true calling. The response of men's hearts to divine destiny must be birthed by the Holy Ghost. Most ministries are not guided exclusively by His Word. There has been little widespread response to the real voice of the Lord. The aftermath of this great vacuum is a maze of confusion with a barnyard full of emphases saying, "This is what God is saying!" It would appear that God has something different in mind on every corner. But the Lord of glory has but *one* theme, message, and project: to build Himself a holy habitation in the earth that will contain and then dispense His glory, a people out of whom He can live and bless the nations. Men must cry out for an up-to-date encounter with God that will rejuvenate this heavenly vision.

A man divinely commissioned and "in" the Lord's message has consistent, predictable results: God will show up! His impartation rings with a single declaration, "I am with you, saith the Lord (Ps. 23:4; Is. 43:2)!" Survival in the last days pivots on two hinges: We must know that the Lord is with us, and we must declare that we are with the Lord (Mt. 1:23; 28:20).

This published revelation transcends circumstances and reconnects our inner being to the divine dream. Jehovah's anointed presence stopped the drought (Hag. 1:11). Apostles and prophets are unfolding the mystery of the Church as the ongoing incarnation of Christ (Eph. 3:1-5;

1 Jn. 2:1-3; 4:17). They bear witness that God is ever-present, enabling us to raise up His house. The holy confidence of being His anointed people requires our commitment to His predetermined objective. God-sent men must be "in" the Lord's message. The message in the prophet is his spiritual heredity—Christ in the man. The prophet in the message is his spiritual environment—the man in Christ. Jesus, the Pattern Son, lived "in" the Father.

The message of the outer court, the Feast of Passover, proclaims Jesus as Savior. The Feast of Pentecost announces Jesus as the One who baptizes with the Holy Ghost. The message of the Most Holy Place, the Feast of Tabernacles, unveils Jesus as King and Lord, "the Lord's message." You might be the Lord's messenger, but are you in the Lord's message? Are you preaching good news or bad news? Are you obsessed with life or death? Jesus or the devil? The new man or the old man?

The Lord's drought brought the remnant to the end of themselves. Only a genuine word from the Lord can accomplish and consummate the divine purpose (Phil. 2:13; Eph. 1:10-11). The dry season brings us back to His voice, rejoins us to His house, and resurrects a living hope (1 Pet. 1:3).

Stirred in the Spirit

Man is a trichotomy, a tripartite or threefold being. Like God, he is a spirit, has a soul, and expresses Himself through a body (1 Thess. 5:23). The *pneuma* or spirit of man is his God-consciousness through five spiritual senses. The *soma* or body of man is his world-consciousness through five natural senses. In the pivotal middle of man is his *psyche* or soul, his self-consciousness, his intellect, emotions, and will—his mind.

2 Cor. 1:10, KJV

Who delivered us from so great a death, and doth deliver: in whom we trust that he will yet deliver us.

Salvation is all-encompassing; it is far more than the new birth (Jn. 3:1-8). The Greek word for "salvation" is *soteria* and means "a complete deliverance." We have been saved, we are being saved, and we shall be saved. When we accepted Jesus Christ as our personal Savior, He raised our spirit from the dead and lit our candle (Prov. 20:27; Jn. 5:24; Eph. 2:1). Man's spirit has been saved. As we progressively grow in grace, there is an on-going transformation of the soul, the renovating of our minds (Rom. 12:1-2; 2 Cor. 3:18). Man's soul is being saved. The salvation experience will climax with the redemption of our body (Rom. 8:19-23; Phil. 3:21). Man's body will be saved. Salvation is past, present, and future.

In the past, we have reacted in our soul through the mind of the flesh; we have been governed by sense knowledge, the passing realm of appearances—the temporal realm of death. Now we are learning to respond in our spirit through the mind of the Spirit, to be governed by the knowledge of the Word of God, the permanent realm of real faith—the eternal realm of spirit.

Hag. 1:14, KJV

And the Lord stirred up the spirit of Zerubbabel the son of Shealtiel, governor of Judah, and the spirit of Joshua the son of Josedech, the high priest, and the spirit of all the remnant of the people; and they came and did work in the house of the Lord of hosts, their God.

Hag. 1:14-15, TLB

And the Lord gave them a desire to rebuild his Temple; so they all gathered in early September of the second year of King Darius' reign and volunteered their help.

Only the Lord can awaken the inner man. Without Him, we can do nothing (Jn. 15:5). Only a messenger sent from God *in* the Lord's message can move his generation. The Lord stirred up the "spirit" of Zerubbabel, Joshua, and all the remnant of the people. This is the Hebrew word *ruach*, meaning "breath, air, wind, strength, breeze, spirit, courage, temper, Spirit." It complements the Greek word *pneuma*. Its primitive root can mean "to smell or perceive; figuratively, to anticipate, enjoy." Haggai's words broke through, inspiring the heart of his congregation.

The word for "stirred" in Haggai 1:14 means "to wake (through the idea of opening the eyes); stir up, rouse oneself" and comes from a primitive root meaning "to be bare, to be made naked." Occurring approximately 80 times in Scripture, its first mention is in Judges 5:12. This word is used in Ezra 1:15 to describe the rousing of King Cyrus to action and the initial awakening of the remnant to return to Jerusalem. For fifteen years the sleep of negligence had interrupted the primary vision. The "Lord's messenger in the Lord's message" was the right medicine, the eyesalve of fresh faith.

God uses prophets to stir our nest, to prepare us to ascend like the eagle (Deut. 32:11-12). In these days of harvest, the firstfruits are awaking early (Ps. 57:8). Once again, the Church will have the tongue of the learned (Is. 50:4). The eyes of our understanding, literally, "the eyes of our heart" or spirit, are being enlightened (Eph. 1:18; Is. 52:1). Once the remnant resolved to hear the Word of the Lord in their hearts, they went back to "work." This word in verse fourteen means "deputyship or ministry; employment (never servile); work; property (as the result of labor)." Its root is the same word as "messenger" in verse thirteen.

The spiritual awakening took place among a "remnant," not among the majority who stayed in Babylon. Our generation must appreciate its critical stretch of Church history. A fresh voice from the Lord has been birthed in the earth (1 Sam. 3:19-21). Real prophets are rallying us to divine purpose. Resurrected expectation will direct us to a future that really contains His heart. It's time to go back to work. Until there is a latter house of greater glory marked by unbreakable relationships, every other accomplishment will be inferior. The specific thing that God has set for our lives is our contribution toward building His House. True success cannot be found in anything else. What will it take to make us see that? How many times must we frustrate ourselves with lesser things?

The overwhelming state of today's temple cannot be faced without a real messenger in the real message. Stop wallowing in the dusty discouragement of human premonition ("Philistine" means "to roll in the dust"). Goliath is a menacing figure, but he will fall by the word of the indwelling Christ, the hidden man after God's own heart (Acts 13:22; 1 Pet. 3:4)! God's higher purpose is for you and your family to be incorporated into His permanent Sanctuary as genuine joints of supply (Eph. 4:16). That spiritual operation transcends the routine of showing up for meetings and giving money. It necessitates knowing that our heart is the foreordained place from which God lives as an abiding reality. Believe God, believe in His Church (Jn. 14:1). Break the yoke of negativism. Stir yourself with new passion and zeal for the work of the Lord. These are days of great opportunity. Be found joined to His people, not operating your own agenda. Turn your heart again.

Don't be disqualified from His vision by removing your influence from the house of the Lord. The Lord has preserved and kept us by the power of His own faith (1 Pet. 1:5). We are not committed to just a small part of this vision, but to the bigger picture: a house of quality and glory greater than that of any previous generation.

Can God still stir you? Can He arouse and provoke you? Can you lay your facade down, all the busyness, your sweaty preoccupation with all that is going in your "house"? Can you surrender your individual motives for the corporate vision? Are you willing to become a contributing member of His Body? Are you ready to commit to what Jesus Christ originally called you to be and to do?

Sovereigns, Saviors, and Survivors

There is a prophetic army of kings and priests in the earth, a many-membered Haggai. We are the Lord's messengers in the Lord's message, willing ambassadors with a *resolve* to hear and obey His Word. God has stirred our "spirits" and awakened our hearts to hear present truth. We have eaten the honey; our eyes have been enlightened (1 Sam. 14:27).

Like Zerubbabel, we are kings or *sovereigns;* we have been given authority. Like Joshua, we are priests or *saviors* (Obad. 1:21). Filled with mercy and compassion, we have an awareness of human need. Like the remnant, we are *survivors*. Our experiences in being brought to this day have qualified us with the ability to get the job done. We can reach out to others because we know what God has done to comfort us (2 Cor. 1:3-5). The devil gave it his best shot, and failed! We are sovereigns, saviors, and survivors... with supernatural authority, awareness, and ability.

The most effective weapon that satan utilizes to stifle the saints is the remembrance of sins, their past mistakes. But we have been accepted and forgiven in the Beloved; His blood has removed our transgressions and turned our captivity (Eph. 1:6-7). Our most effective spiritual weapon is to understand that we are *survivors*, kept by His faith and power. The tables have been turned (Hag. 2:22): Haman has been hung on his own gallows (Esther 7:10). What used to be the devil's advantage is now our greatest asset; we have our *ability* to minister to others because we know that God has taken care of us! He made a way and brought us through (Ps. 124; Rom. 8:31; 1 Pet. 1:5).

We have the ability to reach our generation. Whom He calls, He equips. His biddings are His enablings. Arise and build!

A Quick Work

Hag. 1:1, KJV

In the second year of Darius the king, in the sixth month, in the first day of the month, came the word of the Lord by Haggai the prophet...

Hag. 1:15, KJV

In the four and twentieth day of the sixth month, in the second year of Darius the king.

Once God finds a prophet to speak His Word and a people who respond to the heavenly vision, He does a quick work. He restores the years (Joel 2:25).

Haggai had begun his message on the first day of the sixth month. Now, just three weeks later, God began to move! What the cankerworm had eaten over 15 years was restored in just 23 days! The sixth month was a month of harvesting, a time when urgent tasks in the orchards and fields would have to be completed. This interval was also spent in planning and preparing for reconstruction by removing debris and gathering material. Twenty-three days would allow that work to be finished, after which every able-bodied man could be expected to report to the temple site.

If a nation can be born in one day, what can God do in 23 days (Is. 66:8)? In prophesying of these days, the apostle captures the essence of this truth.

Rom. 9:28, KJV

For He will finish the work, and cut it short in righteousness: because a short work will the Lord make upon the earth.

Rom. 9:28, NIV

For the Lord will carry out His sentence on earth with speed and finality.

The Greek word for "finish" is *sunteleo* and describes God's completed purposes in total harmony and cooperation with His creation. The word for "work" is *logos*, translated in John 1:1,14 as the "Word" of God. The completion of His Word will be "cut short" in righteousness. This word *suntemno* emphasizes the concept of one quick blow with His hand. It reveals the singleness and simplicity that is in Christ and the rending of the veil (2 Cor. 3:13-18; 11:2). The "Lord" does this quick work. This is the Greek *kurios* which means "supreme in authority; controller; by implication, Mr. (as a respectful title)." It is translated in the King James Version as "God, Lord, master, Sir." The Church has forgotten its manners, especially at the table of the Lord (1 Cor. 11:23-30). God's promises are "yes" and "amen" (2 Cor. 1:20), but we have forgotten how to address His Majesty as "Yes, Sir."

Jesus is Boss on this job. Let's trade our hard heads for hard hats and get back to the work site. When we do, let's be sure to see the Building from the Father's perspective. The house may not look like much, but "this place" (Hag. 2:9) is about to be filled with the greater glory of unshakeable peace!

Part Two

The Parameter of Unshakeable Peace— The Whole Earth!

Chapter Five

The Remembrance

"How do you see it now?"

Haggai 2:1-5

Haggai's debut had proven most effective. God reclaimed fifteen years of unbelief and procrastination in just 23 days! Once men *resolve* to hear God's prophet, they can no longer postpone the burden of divine purpose. The remnant had considered their ways and resumed the work on the temple. Nearly a month later, Haggai was given another word from the Lord. During the interim, concentrated efforts had cleared the site of rubble, redressed stones that were fit for use, tested for safety the walls that yet remained, and organized teams of workmen for particular tasks. This rigor taxed even the most enthusiastic, thus the need for encouragement. Besides, progress would have become delayed during the seventh month by the major festivals when no work would be allowed.

The Festival of Ingathering finally arrived, but this usually joyous week had been rather sad...the harvest had dismally failed (Hag. 1:6-11; 2:16). To rebuild the temple in such hard times seemed hopeless. The moment was festive, but fathers and mothers who had seen the magnificence of the previous temple were not pleased (1 Chron. 22:5). Zerubbabel's temple would never match Solomon's. No skilled craftsmen had come from abroad, and the interior was not covered with gold (1 Kings 6:21-22). This second temple was inferior, with little to show for work already performed. The younger generation was glad to see any measure of restoration, but the ancient men wept when they *remembered* Zion (Ezra 3:12; Ps. 137). These unfavorable comparisons between the present and the past would undermine all incentive to persevere. The fervor of some had grown cold again, and malcontents, who had perhaps held themselves aloof from the beginning, found ready listeners. Why not quit work? Haggai discerned that the enterprise was threatened unless the Lord could revive their former courage and enthusiasm. He had little sympathy for nostalgia. Prophets have a way of making men face the reality of the present.

The First Glory

The first sight of Jerusalem in 536 B.C. must have been a keen disappointment to Zerubbabel and his friends. Once the object of Judah's praise (Ps. 48), its proud walls were masses of litter, its gates scorched, its temple a mound of blackened stones and ashes, its streets overgrown with weeds. Now, fifteen years later, the pioneers were haunted by another frustrating scene: a lonely altar on a lonelier foundation, an empty sanctuary that cried out to be finished and filled.

Hag. 2:1, KJV

In the seventh month, in the one and twentieth day of the month, came the word of the Lord by the prophet Haggai, saying,

Hag. 2:1, TLB

In early October of the same year, the Lord sent them this message through Haggai.

The date of Haggai's second prophecy is most significant. The "seventh month" is Tishri, covering the latter part of September and the first part of October. The twenty-first day of the seventh month is the last day of the Feast of Tabernacles, which began on the fifteenth and lasted for seven days (Lev. 23:33-44). One month later, Zechariah's voice would confirm the message of his predecessor (Zech. 1:1).

The fall harvest is the singular reason for observing the Feast of Ingathering (Lev. 23:39). But the Jewish remnant was acclaiming the Feast of Booths without the reality of a crop (Hag. 1:6,9)! We have done the same. Everywhere, there is festivity without manifestation. The message announcing the third feast in the "Third Day" has become a heavyweight theology with lightweight results. The current emphasis upon Tabernacles, without the actuality of glory and ingathering, is alarming. We have not experienced the genuine harvest of:

1. *The evangelization of all men and nations.*

2. *The abundance of the fruit of the Spirit, the divine nature, in the lives of all saints.*

First, church growth in America is like an aquarium full of all kinds of fish. We flop from tank to tank, content to swim in circles until the next feeding. Furthermore, there has been no bona fide glory cloud because the temple, the Body of Christ, is immature and incomplete. Thus we have a dual dilemma: Senior saints longingly *remember* the former revivals of Azuza Street (1906) and North Battleford (1948), and the rest of us have never witnessed a generational move of God.

Hag. 2:2, KJV

Speak now to Zerubbabel the son of Shealtiel, governor of Judah, and to Joshua the son of Josedech, the high priest, and to the residue of the people, saying.

Hag. 2:2, NIV

"Speak to Zerubbabel son of Shealtiel, governor of Judah, to Joshua son of Jehozadak, the high priest, and to the remnant of the people. Ask them."

The word for "residue" here is the same as "remnant" in Haggai 1:12,14, and means "a remainder or residual (surviving, final) portion." God always leaves a trace of Himself in every generation. His purpose in restoring the Tabernacle of David is to gather "the residue of men" from all nations (Acts 15:17). The prophet now poses a heart-piercing question, a direct challenge to make the remnant face the reality of their present condition.

Hag. 2:3, KJV

Who is left among you that saw this house in her first glory? and how do ye see it now? is it not in your eyes in comparison of it as nothing?

Hag. 2:3, NIV

Who of you is left who saw this house in its former glory? How does it look to you now? Does it not seem to you like nothing?

Who is "left" among you? This is the root word for "remnant" or "residue." Who is alive and remaining (1 Thess. 4:17)? Who has survived the days of religious confusion? Who hasn't burned out? For the word "house" in verse three, see Haggai 1:2. Don't despise the day of small things (Zech. 4:9-10). Even in its wasted state, "this house" was still His house! The "first" glory means "first in place, time, or rank; former, chief" and is taken from the Hebrew root for "head." It is translated in the King James Version as "beginning; captain, chief, ruler." Historically, the temple in its "first glory" was the temple Solomon constructed primarily of pure gold (1 Kings 6:20-21). Spiritually, the house in its "first glory" recounts our conversion, our beginnings in Passover, the new birth (Ex. 12:2; Jn. 3:7). Our earliest taste of divine glory came when Jesus *first* saved us, when He was "Head" and "Chief" of our hearts (Rev. 2:4).

Has there ever been a time in your walk when your affection for the Lord was more intense? Your prayer life, Bible study, witness to others, your love for the House of God or His people...was there ever a time when the passion, the fire, was greater? How do you see it now? Recapture that moment, that singleness of heart. Jesus must have the first dominion (Mic. 4:8; Mt. 6:33). Repair the altar; then go on to know the Lord.

The time of "first glory" can also pertain to the out-pouring of the Spirit in the Latter Rain revival of 1948-1956. Older saints who *remember* those days of genuine glory and power can easily fall prey to discouragement. They readily discern the shallowness of contemporary Christianity, the current emphasis on Tabernacles without a real harvest. "Third Day" conferences are chic, marked by jubilation without substance. In a frenzy of flesh, others try for hours to conjure up the cloud the size of a man's hand without the prophet, the altar, or the fire (1 Kings 18:19-29). But if we will build it, He will come. Elijah's altar pictures a lamb company repaired, then prepared for sacrifice. Much of our current celebration is premature.

Part of our famine has been the woeful lack of Pentecostal theologians, men of the Word (Amos 8:11-14). Spiritual neophytes are sloganizing the saints to death with cute sayings and proof texts that cannot feed the inner man (2 Tim. 4:3-4). Clever clichés from the tree of knowledge are sorry substitutes for godly wisdom from the Tree of life, the Word of God. Paul, a wise master-builder in Bible exegesis and exposition, said it best, "Preach the Word..." (2 Tim. 4:2).

Jn. 7:37, KJV

In the last day, that great day of the feast, Jesus stood and cried, saying, If any man thirst, let him come unto Me....

John the beloved reveals our Lord as the living Word. The seventh chapter of his Gospel is a panorama of the

Feast of Tabernacles in the life of Jesus. While the Pharisees enjoyed going through the motions of ritual and ceremony, the Lord of the harvest was noticeably absent from their liturgy. The "last day" of the last feast is to be sanctified by great joy, and it is yet to be realized by the Church. In that critical season of genuine glory, preachers will not be running to their own houses, nor God's people to the rich and famous. The gathering, the whole Feast, will be unto Him!

How Do You See It Now?

Sixty-six years had elapsed since the destruction of Solomon's temple. The aged men in Haggai's audience would have been small children when Nebuchadnezzar besieged and burned Jerusalem (586 B.C.). According to *Vine's*, the word for "see" in Haggai 2:3 means "to see, observe, perceive, get acquainted with, gain understanding, examine, look after (see to), choose, discover."

What is your point of view? Perspective determines perception. The true spiritual state of things can only be discerned and understood by the Spirit. In Ezekiel 8–9, the prophet was taken in the visions of God and shown the inward condition of the temple. We must "see" from the heavenlies; men will never consider their ways until they rediscover the divine posture (Song 4:8; Eph. 2:6; Phil. 3:20).

Hag. 2:3, NIV

Who of you is left who saw this house in its former glory? How does it look to you now? Does it not seem to you like nothing?

The latter inquiry probes the heart. The Revised Version reads, "Is it not in your eyes as nothing?" Those who participated in the reality of the Pentecostal and Latter Rain Revivals would have to honestly respond, "Yes. All this today seems like nothing." God has come to renew our valor and fervor. How can we who were never part of a former glory relate to Haggai's questions? Many who lived through those days have given up; they see no spiritual structure on the planet, no wineskin capable of receiving the fullness of His peace and glory. No local church, no group, no camp or stream is presently set up to contain or dispense His promised outpouring. The revival in the Book of Acts was but a beginning portion "out of" all that Joel predicted (Joel 2:28; Acts 2:17)!

The post-exilic Jews were celebrating their scanty crop that had survived the drought (Hag. 1:6,9,11). The harvest today is a far cry from the real Feast of Tabernacles. Every ministry has fallen short of that glory. Brethren, our vision is too small. There's a real work to be done. We are not one...yet (Hag. 2:6; Eph. 4:13).

Current circumstances have caused pastors and leaders to burn up or burn out. Some have been pressed out of full-time ministry and back into secular work. We must not allow a cynical evaluation of negative things to derail us and drive away our influence from the house of God. Many escape facing the facts by lingering at the altar of hyper-dispensationalism. In the last 150 years, the any-minute, pre-tribulation rapture theory has become an American icon. The issue is not eschatological, but governmental. Who's in charge, God's Word or cherished tradition? The Bible emphasizes His coming, not our going...His appearing, not our disappearing. Jesus the Prophet recounted Noah's day when the wicked were taken and the righteous were left to inherit the earth (Mt. 24:37-41)!

Prov. 10:30, KJV

The righteous shall never be removed....

The any-minute rapture teaching, like Jeroboam's private invention, counterfeits the Feast of Tabernacles (1 Kings 12:32-33). The pre-tribulation view is popular because one can reign without suffering. The only requirement to be "out of here on the first load" is to be born again. What effrontery to the apostles' doctrine!

First of all, the Church is Abraham's Seed, the true Israel of God (see Rom. 2:28-29; 9:6-8; Gal. 3-4; 6:16). New Testament believers are the spiritual circumcision, the heavenly Jerusalem, God's chosen people, the holy Nation (Phil. 3:3; Heb. 12:22-23; 1 Pet. 2:9). Bible theology is covenantal. The law, not the Church, was parenthetical. We're not second-class citizens, not Gentiles (*ethnos*, the Greek word meaning "pagan, heathen"). Jesus secured the promises made to the patriarchal fathers (Acts 3:13; Rom. 15:8); He and His Church are the Seed of Abraham and David (Mt. 1:1; Eph. 2:11-12).

Second, Jesus Christ, not some future antichrist, was the "Prince" who caused the sacrifice and oblation to cease at the cross after three-and-one-half years of ministry; His offering was once-and-for-all (Dan. 9:24-27; Heb. 8–10). The whole dispensational scheme rests on Daniel's prophecy of seventy weeks. Much of Matthew 24,

Luke 21, and the Book of Revelation has been historically fulfilled.

Third, we're not ready to meet the Lord. The real temple is incomplete, destined for three feasts, not one or two. The Lord cannot come until His Bride has matured (Ps. 110:1; Heb. 10:12-13). Jesus has sent a fivefold team of architects to build and perfect His house (1 Cor. 3:10; Gal. 4:1-2; Eph. 4:11-16). He must remain in Heaven until His Church is restored and times of refreshing and glory have come from His presence (Acts 3:19-21).

Historically, the Feast of Trumpets began in February of 1948. Over 40 years later, the Day of the Lord has dawned; the trumpet has become an alarm (Joel 2:1). On one hand, many leaders are but children playing in the streets, piping to one another. On the other, there are ten thousand top-heavy instructors with great communication skills, but no power to set the captives free. Meanwhile, God's house is halfway finished. How do you see it now?

God is taking issue with movements. Every tribe has been infected with a spirit of dejection and discontent. Every denomination and non-denominational denomination has its own golden calf. The Master of the house is going after every current emphasis to bring alteration to each and every one of them. Jesus has come to cleanse His temple, to adjust our vision (Hag. 2:22). We have been so absorbed in getting the glory to come that we have forgotten to build and become the thing that will contain it. Many have fainted, disallowing that such a structure can be produced out of the present situation. Such alibis grow out of one's shortage of reality with regard to the house of God. Behind every excuse is a lack of desire.

Novices jumping on the bandwagon of present truth have yet to walk through the furnace, the baptism of fire. Sonship is costly (Dan. 3:25). To presumptuous men, the Feast of Tabernacles is but another hot commodity, a fad to market, a wave to ride. The number one error among adolescent leadership is an inclination to preach a "Third Day" message while maintaining second day agendas. The meager crop of such folly is religious hype—a lot of flashy noise with little change of heart. But God is marking intercessors who grieve and lament detestable things (Ezek. 9:4). Those most concerned with the Church's present state will make the greatest impact in coming days. While others frolic, we are building a place of safety: the house of the Lord. A flood is coming; there is an approaching sound of abundant rain. Those who are playing with present truth (preaching only enough to be palatable and remain politically correct) just to beef up their numbers will soon be banging on the door of the ark.

Reconnect to God's original vision. Stir up the gift. You are part of a heavenly family, a member in particular. Be established in your unique gifting and calling. Your predestined contribution is necessary to the triumphant fulfillment of divine purpose.

The Glory of the Lord

Despite our ignorance and obvious weaknesses, God has promised to pour out His glory. The word for "glory" in Haggai 2:3 (compare Hag. 1:8 and 2:7,9) is *kabowd*

(Strong's #3519) and it means "weight; splendor or copious-ness; honor." The primitive root *kabad* (Strong's #3513) means "to be heavy; numerous, rich, honorable." This word, found over 200 times in biblical Hebrew, can also mean "great quantity, multitude, wealth, reputation, majesty."

Kabowd refers to the great physical weight or "quan-tity" of a thing (Is. 22:24). This "glory" often refers to both "wealth" and significant or positive "reputation" (Gen. 31:1; 45:13). It carries the idea of richness and abun-dance (Ps. 85:12), royal presence and position (1 Sam. 4:21). When used in the sense of "honor" or "impor-tance" (Gen. 45:13), there are two particulars. First, *kabowd* can emphasize the position and relationships of an individual within his sphere (Prov. 11:16; 20:3; 25:2). Second, nobility is suggested, such as "honor" that belongs to a royal family (1 Kings 3:13). When applied to God, "glory" represents a quality corresponding to Him and by which He is recognized (Josh. 7:19). *Kabowd* also points to divine sovereignty over history, specifically, to a future exhibition of that glory (Is. 40:5). Other passages relate the manifestation of divine glory to past demon-strations of His reign over history and peoples (Ex. 16:7; 24:16). The adjective of "glory" means "heavy; numer-ous; severe; rich" and occurs about 40 times in Scripture. It carries the connotation of heaviness as an enduring, ever-present quality, a lasting thing. Used positively, it describes "riches" (Gen. 13:2).

All the aforementioned qualities of "glory" center in Jesus Christ, and describe the end-time Church con-formed to His image (Jn. 1:14; 17:22). Volumes could be written about the glory that fills the latter house. Con-sider these thoughts from the Book of Exodus:

1. *The glory appeared in the cloud (Ex. 16:10).*

2. *God spoke out of the glory (Ex. 24:16).*

3. *Aaron's garments were for glory (Ex. 28:40).*

4. *The tent was sanctified by glory (Ex. 29:43).*

5. *Moses saw the glory (Ex. 33:18-22).*

6. *The glory filled Moses' Tabernacle (Ex. 40:34-35).*

The "glory" of the Lord is most prominently used in the Book of Psalms (see Ps. 8:5; 19:1; 72:19; 102:16; 145:11) and the Book of Isaiah (see Is. 4:5; 6:3; 35:2; 40:5; 60:1-2). Other key verses are Numbers 14:21, Second Chronicles 7:3, Ezekiel 1:28; 43:2, Habakkuk 2:14, and Zechariah 2:5.

Do you *remember* the first glory? How do you see it "now" or "at this time"? For the remnant, the restored temple seemed as "nothing" or a non-entity when compared to the temple of Solomon. This word in Haggai 2:3 is translated in the King James Version as "fail, fatherless, be gone, incurable." God now comes to rejuvenate our spirit. But can He bring such glory from the present ruin of an orphaned sanctuary? We cry out, "Lord, will it ever happen?"

Be Strong

Jesus promised that He would not leave us comfortless (Jn. 14:18); He would send the power of the Holy Spirit. Likewise, Jehovah restored the remnant's confidence in His continued presence. Most discouragement is rooted in the lack of that reality. Haggai addresses the leaders first. They were to be strong, proving their worth and accountability.

Much of the present hoopla over the Feast of Tabernacles is as nothing. Having witnessed much human effort from a myriad of streams trying to produce spiritual realities, I have become a candidate for encouragement. Our courage has been low because of what we have seen. We have not been discouraged with the Lord but with the work of the Lord. So we cry to know His will: a real work to be done and a God who is really involved in that work. Many are hesitant to reengage their heart with God or His people. Their peace has been shaken. Relationships lie crumbled, shattered by disillusionment. I personally know scores of people all over America who have simply quit. These hearts gradually deteriorated, not with the personal giving of themselves to the Lord, but to His work.

Each of us must ask, "Is there an honest witness of the Holy Spirit upon what I am doing? Is it coming out of a true result of harvest that God has produced?" We can become confident again. The Lord is with us!

Hag. 2:4, KJV

Yet now be strong, O Zerubbabel, saith the Lord; and be strong, O Joshua, son of Josedech, the high priest; and be strong, all ye people of the land, saith the Lord, and work: for I am with you, saith the Lord of hosts.

Hag. 2:4, AMP

Yet now be strong, alert, and courageous....

Hag. 2:4, Knox

...the Lord of hosts bids you put heart into the work—is not He, the Lord of hosts, at your side?

This word for "strong" means "to fasten upon; hence, to seize, be strong or courageous; causatively, to strengthen, cure, help, repair, fortify; to bind restrain, conquer." This verb is found 290 times in the Old Testament. Joshua and Solomon received the admonition to "be strong" (Josh. 1:6-9; 1 Chron. 22:13; 28:20), and Zechariah confirmed Haggai's encouraging words (Zech. 8:9). Compare the similar New Testament inspiration from the apostle Paul (Eph. 6:10; 2 Tim. 2:1).

1 Cor. 16:13, NIV

Be on your guard; stand firm in the faith; be men of courage; be strong.

Be bold to finish the "work" of the Lord. This Hebrew word in Haggai 2:4 means "to do or make; create" and is translated as "bring forth, be busy, execute, fulfill, govern, labour, perform, provide" in the King James Version. There is a threefold admonition in verse four. This declaration is made to Zerubbabel, Joshua, and the remnant (compare Hag. 2:14). Be strong...in divine authority, awareness, and ability! Be strong in Passover, be strong in Pentecost, be strong in Tabernacles. Be strong...as a babe, a youth, a man. Be strong...in spirit, soul, and body. Overcoming Christians are strong in the Lord and the power of His might (Eph. 6:10). The prophet then reveals his source of confidence: "I am with you, saith the Lord of hosts" (Hag. 2:4).

Jehovah had assured His remnant earlier (Hag. 1:13). David, Joseph, the apostles of the Lamb, and Paul received the same word of comfort (see 1 Sam. 16:18; 2 Sam. 5:10; Mk. 16:20; Acts 7:9; 2 Tim. 4:17). He who sent us is with us. Haggai's exhortation is a striking parallel to the words of Jesus that stormy night on the lake (Mk. 6:50). The presence of the Lord gives courage and determination, the conviction that His cause will prevail (Is. 35:4). Jesus' name or nature is *Immanuel*, "God with us." He will never leave or forsake us. Haggai continues to jog the remnant's memory, recounting the panoramic description of God's delivering power from the tyranny of Pharaoh. *Remember* the Passover.

When You Came Out of Egypt

Deut. 6:23, KJV

And he brought us out from thence, that he might bring us in....

This ancient promise has always been His commitment to those called to be His permanent dwelling-place (Rom. 11:29). Moses brought them out. Joshua brought them in. God calls His people out by the *hand* of a shepherd that He might bring them in by the *word* of a soldier. Almost a millennium had passed since the establishment of the Mosaic Covenant. Generations had come and gone, but Jehovah's Word remained unchanged. Every generation had heard the Aaronic blessing, which would again be spoken twice daily in the house they were rebuilding (Num. 6:24-26).

Like the remnant, preachers today are paralyzed with fear, panicking and praying out of distress, "Lord, have I lost something in You? Has something drained from my life so that I cannot recapture my love for Your work?

Have I lost my heart for Your people?" We don't fear going back to Egypt's bondage. But for those still hurting from previous relationships, the thought of opening their heart again is quite disturbing. Many have digressed into stagnation and overpowering apprehension, even depression. This gradual slump of courage to stay close to the work of the Lord has come about by personal discouragement with the state of things, including our dismay with the message we are most committed to—the Feast of Tabernacles. When present truth becomes man-centered, contaminated with greed and a desire to be seen, it has the pitiful ring of sounding brass.

The message of Tabernacles and the Most Holy Place is true. Our heart must be reassured that His Spirit is still in covenant with us and with what He has called us to do. Our spirit must be infected with new inspiration, resurrected from previous disappointments. We must release the past, forgive everyone for everything, and go on with God. Every true leader must fearlessly declare these things by precept and life style if God's people are to have real hope. Haggai was faithful to his generation.

Hag. 2:5, KJV

According to the word that I covenanted with you when ye came out of Egypt, so My spirit remaineth among you: fear ye not.

Hag. 2:5, TLB

For I promised when you left Egypt that My Spirit would remain among you; so don't be afraid.

The post-exilic Jews could return to their task without worry. According to the same "word" promised in the Exodus, *Jehovah-Tsebaoth* would now spur on the remnant (Ex. 3:12). This term means "a matter or thing; a cause." Its root means "to arrange, speak; to subdue." That Passover "word" was brought into Pharaoh's court by the king-priest ministry of Moses and Aaron, then confirmed by signs, wonders, and miracles. Its essence was, "Let My people go." Passover is a vast subject, related in threes:

1. *The Passover of Salvation (Ex. 12).*

2. *The Passover of Conquest (Josh. 5).*

3. *The Passover of the Kingdom (Lk. 22)*

Our walk began with the blood of the Lamb (Jn. 1:29). Christ our Passover has been sacrificed for us; His precious blood has brought the forgiveness of sins (1 Cor. 5:7-8; 1 Pet. 1:18-19). This experience marks the "beginning of months" for the believer (Ex. 12:1-3). Subsequently, we received the power of God in our Pentecostal baptism (Acts 1:8). The heavenlies, like Canaan, opened to us in the Passover of conquest (Josh. 5). Our hearts were circumcised and the reproach of the world rolled away at Gilgal; our diet changed from manna to corn (Heb. 6:1-2) and we encountered a new dimension of spiritual warfare. The Captain of our salvation has come to bring down every wall (Eph. 2:14). Ultimately, God's people will pass over into another age. A nation will be born in a day, and the wealth of the nations will come into the Church. Sin and satan will be cut off completely, and men will be freed from the bondage of futility and corruption. God's people will be gloriously delivered (Rom. 8:14-23).

"Let My people go...." This is the heart-cry of the Father for the glorious Church. He has envisioned a vast company of sons, the many-membered Body of Christ. The Body is His permanent abode, each member released by the living Word and a global shaking to make full proof of his ministry. Unshakeable peace spells unbreakable relationships, contracts that cannot be shaken or broken. To this end, God has "covenanted" with us. This word in Haggai 1:5 is *karath* (Strong's #3772) and means "to cut; to covenant; to make an alliance or bargain, originally by cutting flesh and passing between the pieces." *Vine's* adds that *karath* means "to cut off, cut down, fell, cut or make (a covenant or agreement)." In biblical Hebrew it is attested about 290 times and in all periods. God had made a covenant with Israel at Sinai, and would keep His Word (see Ex. 6:7; 19:5-6; 33:12-14; 34:10).

"Egypt" is the world, the place of sin and bondage. It means "a limit; something hemming in; figuratively, distress," and comes from a primitive root meaning "to cramp or confine." The latter is rendered as "adversary, assault, besiege, bind, inclose" in the King James Version. The Passover Lamb came to deliver us from the works of the devil. Jesus overcame the world and all that is in it (1 Jn. 2:15-17; 3:8). God alone can bring us out of that horrible pit, through the wilderness, and into the promised land—His completed Temple of mature sons (Eph. 4:13). There is a difference between the *bondage* of Egypt and the *captivity* of Babylon. The former is past; we have been set free from sin and satan. God's people have not returned to the bondage of Egypt, but our idolatry has kept us bound in religious confusion. Let us return unto the Lord. The One who released us from oppression is with us to finish what He began (Jn. 16:33; 1 Jn. 5:4-5).

Our boldness rests in this: His Spirit "remains" or "stands" among us...He abides. *Vine's* adds that this word in Haggai 2:5 means "to take one's stand; stand here or be there; stand still." The Hebrew participle denotes continuous action and includes both past and present within its meaning. God *was* with His people, and God *is* with His people! In Christ, we are steadfast and immovable, resting in His never-failing peace. His Spirit stands "among" us. This Hebrew root means "to sever; a bisection, the center; midst or middle." The King and His Kingdom is "among" us, in our midst. His good Spirit rests upon us to instruct us, to reveal the Son (Neh. 9:20; Jn. 16:13). His abiding presence has freed us from "fear." This word in verse five means "to fear; morally, to revere, stand in awe; to frighten." Compare Haggai 1:12 and Zechariah 8:13-15. Fear, like faith, has a voice. Faith comes by meditating on the Word of the Lord; fear comes by considering the suggestions of the enemy (Is. 41:10).

God's Spirit is at work. The Lord is in His holy temple (Hab. 2:20). His anointing abides, impacting our placement in His army and every measure of ministry. He has not given us the spirit of fear. We will not need to fight in this battle (2 Chron. 20:17). His grace is enough.

Remember the great things the Lord has done. We are about to be *released* into all that He has planned.

Chapter Six

The Release

..."and I will fill this house with glory..."

Haggai 2:6-9

The one true God who brought His people out of Egypt is with us to complete His predetermined purpose. The earth will have its Jubilee, its captives rescued from futility's prisonhouse (Lev. 25; Lk. 4:18-19). All creation is ready for *release*, standing on tiptoe waiting for the sons of God to come into their own (Rom. 8:19-23). Haggai couches this emancipation in terms of the Exodus, Israel's deliverance from Pharaoh and the brickyards of Egypt (Hag. 2:5). The day of shaking is upon us! Everything is shifting into a higher gear. This global eruption will prove and declare the quality of every man's work. Every ceiled house must pass through the Refiner's fire (Mal. 3:1-3; 1 Cor. 3:9-15). Casual tremors, indicators of greater shakings, have already begun to upset us. The apostle Peter predicted a universal convulsion in the last chapter of his second epistle, divulging three worlds (2 Pet. 3:6-7,13):

1. *The world that then was. (2 Pet. 3:6)*

2. *The world kept in store until now. (2 Pet. 3:7)*

3. *The world wherein dwells righteousness. (2 Pet. 3:13)*

The Greek word for "world" is *kosmos* (English "cosmetic") and means "an order, system or arrangement of things." The cosmos is a mindset, a mentality, a way of thinking with its consequent life style. The first world was Noah's cosmos. God destroyed that order (not the earth) with *water* (2 Pet. 3:6). In spiritual realities, God consumed our old man, the world that then was, in the waters of baptism (1 Pet. 3:20-21). The second world exists from that time until now, reserved unto *fire*: His Word or Voice in the mouth of His prophets (Jer. 23:29; Heb. 12:29). The elements that melt with fervent heat are the beggarly elements, the rudimentary concepts and principles of man-made tradition (2 Pet. 3:7). The third world, the next world government, is the immovable Kingdom whose government and peace is marked by endless increase (Is. 9:7; 2 Pet. 3:13).

A Kingdom Which Cannot Be Moved

The key passage that inspired this volume nows lies before us. These verses anticipate *unshakeable peace* in the time of global shaking. Throughout the nation and the world, something is astir. Everyone's spiritual instincts sense that something is about to happen. Haggai 2:6-9 is vividly rehearsed in Hebrews 12:25-29 and amazingly paralleled by Ezekiel 37:1-14. We will examine both passages before we continue the exegesis of Haggai.

Heb. 12:25-26, KJV

See that ye refuse not Him that speaketh. For if they escaped not who refused him that spake on earth, much more shall not we escape, if we turn away from Him that speaketh from heaven:

Whose voice then shook the earth: but now He hath promised, saying, Yet once more I shake not the earth only, but also heaven.

The word for "voice" in Hebrews 12:26 is *phone* and means "noise, sound, voice." It is taken from *phaino*, "to shine," and its root *phos*, the word for "light." The light of His Word is certain and powerful, a "voice" that men can hear and see. The word for "shook" and "shake" means "to waver, agitate, rock, topple, or destroy; figuratively, to disturb or incite." Its root means "a vibration; billow," referring to the action of stormy winds or waves; the "sea" symbolizes unsaved multitudes who cannot rest (Is. 57:20). God is sifting out everything without solid foundations (see Mt. 24:29; Lk. 6:48; Acts 4:31; 16:26). This shaking of heaven and earth "signifieth" or "makes plain or clear" the removing of those things that can be shaken—synthetic things.

Heb. 12:27, KJV

And this word, Yet once more, signifieth the removing of those things that are shaken, as of things that are made, that those things which cannot be shaken may remain.

A key word to its context, "removing" is *metathesis* (Strong's #3331), meaning "transposition, transferral (to

Heaven), disestablishment (of a law)." *Vine's* adds, "a change of position." This word is taken from *metatithemi* which means "to transfer, transport, exchange, change sides; to remove a person or thing from one place to another." Unique to Hebrews (Heb. 7:12; 11:5), *metathesis* is rendered in the King James Version as "change, removing, translation." This global shift is a moving experience—from earth to Heaven, from joy to sorrow, from darkness to light, from death to life. We are jarred out of the temporal into the eternal, out of the passing into the permanent, out of the appearance (sight) realm into faith. Things that cannot be moved will "remain" or "abide; stay (in a given place, state, relation, or expectancy)."

Heb. 12:28-29, KJV

> *Wherefore we receiving a kingdom which cannot be moved, let us have grace, whereby we may serve God acceptably with reverence and godly fear:*
> *For our God is a consuming fire.*

Then we shall "receive" the enduring peace of His Kingdom (Rom. 14:17). *Paralambano* means "to receive near, associate with oneself (in any familiar intimate act or relation); to assume an office; figuratively, to learn." *Vine's* adds "to receive from another." This is the peace that He alone can give (Jn. 14:27). Global shaking has begun. Out-of-control climate changes, floods, hurricanes, droughts, fires, earthquakes, and volcanos are the travail of natural creation, the birth-pangs of a new day. God will fill the earth with Himself. Send Your voice, Lord. Shake us until we cannot be moved.

Bones and Stones

Ezek. 37:7, KJV

So I prophesied as I was commanded: and as I prophesied, there was a noise, and behold a shaking, and the bones came together, bone to his bone.

Dry bones lay scattered in the valley like the burnt stones of Zerubbabel's temple. In both settings, the Word of the Lord brought a great "shaking" (the same Hebrew word in Ezekiel 37:7 and Haggai 2:6,7,21). The Hebrew word for "noise" in this verse means "voice." This order is confirmed by Hebrews 12:26—God's Word, His voice, brings the shaking (Ezek. 37:7). Each man saw the *house* of the Lord (Ezek. 37:11; Hag. 2:3). Both visionaries anticipated the end-time upheaval and consequent glory of the remnant Church. Ezekiel saw *Jehovah-Tsebaoth's* army (Eph. 6); Haggai beheld the end-time temple of the Lord (Eph. 2). The priest who became a voice to the captive Jews in Babylon envisioned a valley full of parched, disconnected bones. Haggai was challenged with an unfinished building project that lay buried in garbage while every man ran to his own house (Hag. 1:1-9). The winds of God, blowing mightily through both prophets, brought a sudden noise, a great shaking, and much-needed reconnection.

Who were these bones in Ezekiel's vision? How did they get there? They *died* there…the bones of the house of Israel, the consumed carcasses of an unbelieving generation who wasted in the wilderness (Num. 14:30-35)! Those who stop with Pentecost have been brought out from Egypt but not brought in, delivered from sin but not into the promised rest (Deut. 6:22-23; Heb. 4:9-11). The noisy rattling of waterless bones parallels the predicted shaking to an unbelieving remnant who also settled for partial purpose.

Ezek. 37:9, KJV

Then said He unto me, Prophesy unto the wind, prophesy, son of man, and say to the wind, Thus saith the Lord God; Come from the four winds, O breath, and breathe upon these slain, that they may live.

The Body of Christ is a disjointed army, an incomplete temple in urgent need of repair and reconstruction. There is no open vision in the open valley (1 Sam. 3:1; Ezek. 37:2). Our bones are dry, our hope is lost, and we are cut off from our parts. But the four winds are blowing! Winds that bring discernment, delight, destruction, and Heaven's deluge—winds that resurrect the army of the Lord.

Song 4:16, KJV

Awake, O north wind; and come, thou south; blow upon my garden, that the spices thereof may flow out. Let my beloved come into his garden, and eat his pleasant fruits.

The north wind brings *discernment* and Holy Ghost conviction (Jn. 16:8-11). This cold air blew down from the mountains, biting and killing everything but the evergreens. The only thing that can live in the presence of God is God. Everything outside of Christ is judged and removed by the north wind. The south wind, soft and warm, is the wind of *delight*. The Comforter must come (Jn. 14:26; 15:26). God's disassembled troops will be refreshed by the gentleness of His grace and mercy, the soothing warmth of His Breath upon those slain. Be strong. The Lord of hosts is with you!

Job 1:19, KJV

And, behold, there came a great wind from the wilderness, and smote the four corners of the house....

Lk. 12:54, KJV

And he said also to the people, When ye see a cloud rise out of the west, straightway ye say, There cometh a shower....

The east wind is a severe tempest, the wind of *destruction*. The Holy Ghost is blowing away man-made structures, bringing the sturdiest seaman to his wit's end (Ps. 107:23-27). Those who would rather vote than hear the apostle have one objective—to make it to "haven" before Euroclydon hits (Acts 27:11-20). Their false hope and means of secret escape will soon be tossed to the wind of the wilderness (Acts 27:30-32). Discernment, delight, destruction...are followed by Heaven's *deluge!* The west wind brings showers of blessing, times of refreshing from the presence and glory of the Lord. The four winds have answered the prophet's call. In the third day, His Breath will raise us up, and we shall live in His sight (Hos. 6:2).

This fourfold, universal operation of the Spirit is gusting through Ezekiel's valley. How blow the Winds of God? The Holy Ghost is aligning bones and stones, rejoining us to the original vision. Right now, we are "very dry." But the divine drought has made us desperate to hear the Lord's messenger in the Lord's message (Hag. 1:11-13). In our broken-down spiritual condition, we may not look like much. But yonder...amidst ashes and weeds and burnt stones...lies the long-forgotten, dismembered dream of God's heart: a people of *unshakeable peace*, unbreakable relationships, an army for His glory!

Ezek. 37:3a, KJV

And He said unto me, Son of man, can these bones live?

Ezek. 37:10, KJV

So I prophesied as He commanded me, and the breath came....

Yet Once

Now that we have surveyed Ezekiel's vision of dry bones and examined Hebrews 12:25-29, let us weigh the keynote passage from which the latter verses were taken (Hag. 2:6-9).

Hag. 2:6, KJV

For thus saith the Lord of hosts; Yet once, it is a little while, and I will shake the heavens, and the earth, and the sea, and the dry land.

Hag. 2:6, TLB

For the Lord of Hosts says, "In just a little while I will begin to shake the heavens and earth—and the oceans, too, and the dry land."

"Yet once again" or "once more" God will shake the nations as He did Egypt with the rod of Moses. The word for "once" is *echad* (Strong's #259) and means "untied, one; or (as the ordinal) first." It comes from a primitive root meaning "to unify; figuratively, to collect one's thoughts," and is translated in the King James Version as "alike, altogether, each one, first, one, only." This phrase, "yet once," concisely sums up the Father's ultimate intention, the mystery of His will; it captures the essence of the high priestly prayer of John 17 and the apostolic aim of Ephesians 4...the unity of the Spirit is to become the unity of the faith. "Yet once" could read, "yet one": *one* house filled with *one* God! In that day, God will collect His thoughts and gather together the outcasts of Israel. He will unify and join the sticks of Judah and Ephraim; they will become one in His hand (Ezek. 37:15-28). No schisms or divisions will be found in that army of peacemakers, a people with one mind and judgment (Ps. 133; Eph. 1:9-10).

Unity cannot be created. It can only be kept. All unity intrinsically flows from the intertheistic union between the Father and the Son, and it is based upon the seven absolutes of Ephesians 4:4-6. Jehovah's primary vision for the returning remnant was singular, to build His House. Zerubbabel's temple points to the one new creation Man of the New Covenant. We don't see all things put under that Man's feet "yet," but we do see Jesus, the Pattern Son, the Author and the Developer of our faith (Heb. 2:6-9; 12:1-2). This shaking of the heavens and earth will resurrect His army and *release* all things into one! To the finite, it seems to take forever. To the infinite

One, it is just a "little while" (Ps. 37:10; Jer. 51:33; Heb. 10:37).

The Hebrew word for "shake" in Haggai 2:6,7,21 is *ra'ash* (Strong's #7493), a primitive root meaning "to undulate (as the earth, the sky, or a field of grain), particularly through fear; specifically, to spring (as a locust)." The present move of His Spirit will revive the fear of the Lord. This key word for "shake" is peculiar to the Book of Psalms (Ps. 60:2; 68:8; 77:18), the books of the Major Prophets (see Is. 34:4; Jer. 10:10; 51:29; Ezek. 38:20), and the books of the Minor Prophets (Joel 2:10, 30-32; Nahum 1:5). Compare Matthew 24:29-31, Luke 21:25-27, Acts 2:19, and Revelation 6:1-17; 8:5-12.

Joel 3:16, KJV

> *The Lord also shall roar out of Zion, and utter His voice from Jerusalem; and the heavens and the earth shall shake....*

Haggai's shaking recalls the Exodus. The humbling of proud Egypt by the ten plagues (Ex. 12:7-12) and the destruction of Pharaoh's army in the Red Sea (Ex. 14) are described as a shaking (Ps. 77:15-20). The Song of Moses contains a sevenfold description of being shaken (Ex. 15:14-16). In a similar manner, the overthrow of Babylon preceding Judah's release from exile is described as a shaking of heaven and earth (Jer. 50:46). These two deliverances, the greatest in the Old Testament, forecast our emancipation in Christ.

This quake begins in the "heavens," then echoes in the "earth." From heaven to earth, from spiritual to natural, from God to man—this is the pattern. The

Hebrew word for "heavens" (Hag. 1:10; 2:21) in verse 6 means "to be lofty." Heaven is the *spiritual* realm or abode of God, who is omnipresent Spirit (Jn. 4:23-24). The word for "earth" (Hag. 1:10-11; 2:4,21) means "to be firm; the earth; land." *Vine's* says the "earth" is the temporal scene of human activity, experience, and history. It denotes the entire planet, but it is also used to refer to some of earth's component parts. It also can refer to an area occupied by a nation or tribe. Earth is the *natural* realm. This celestial and terrestrial shaking also moves the "sea." This word comes from an obscure root meaning "to roar; a sea (as breaking in noisy surf); sea, ocean." In the Bible, the sea represents teeming masses of unregenerate humanity (Is. 57:20). Compare Zechariah 9:4,10; 10:11; 14:4,8.

This overturning of all nations is defined more closely in Haggai 2:22 as the complete overthrow and destruction of the throne and strength of all heathen kingdoms. God rocks the heavens, the earth, the sea, and, finally, the "dry land" or "desert," parched or ruined through drought. This word can also mean "to desolate, destroy, kill" and refers to waste areas. The Bible clearly defines the "dry land" to be rebellion and wickedness (Ps. 68:6; Ezek. 30:12). The heavens, the earth, the sea, the dry land...every thing spiritual and natural, all human rebellion and wickedness, every area of our lives and ministries— define the *parameter* and scope of unshakeable peace.

Hag. 2:7, KJV

And I will shake all nations, and the desire of all nations shall come: and I will fill this house with glory, saith the Lord of hosts.

Hag. 2:7, NIV

...and the desired of all nations will come....

Hag. 2:7, TLB

...and the Desire of All Nations shall come to this Temple....

Hag. 2:7, NKJ

...and they shall come to the Desire of All Nations....

Hag. 2:7, ASV

...and the precious things of all nations shall come....

Nothing is immune. *All* nations are impacted by this worldwide shaking (see Ezek. 21:27; Dan. 2:44-45; 7:20-25; Joel 3:9-16; Lk. 21:10-11). God will shake all "nations" in at least three spheres:

1. *The nations.*

2. *The denominations.*

3. *The imaginations.*

This word for "all" in Haggai 2:7 means "the whole; all, any, or every (often in a plural sense); altogether." It comes from a primitive root which means "to complete" and is translated in the King James Version as "make perfect." This reiterates the *purpose* of unwavering peace: He shakes "all" to make us complete. Overviewing the Book of Haggai, we see that Jehovah shakes:

1. *All the labor (Hag. 1:11).*

2. *All the remnant of the people (Hag. 1:12,14).*

3. *All the people of the land (Hag. 2:4).*

4. *All the nations (Hag. 2:7).*

5. *All of these (Hag. 2:12-13).*

6. *All the works of their hands (Hag. 2:14,17).*

God viewed the Jewish remnant as uncircumcised (Mt. 5:45); the word used in verse seven for "nations" (Hag. 2:14,22) means a "foreign nation; hence, a gentile; people, heathen." It refers to a "people or nation," usually with overtones of territorial or governmental unity or identity. Following Haggai's era, *Jehovah-Tsebaoth* would shake Persia, Greece, and Rome. In recent years, He has shaken the Communist nations and our own. This shaking of all nations has a singular result: the *Desire* of all nations shall come! The Hebrew word for "desire" in Haggai 2:7 is *chemdah* (Strong's #2532). It means "delight, long for, covet" and is translated in the King James Version as "desire, goodly, pleasant, precious." The verb has the sense of choosing (Is. 53:2). This word is used to describe:

1. *The king (1 Sam. 9:20).*

2. *Stones and jewels (2 Chron. 27:32).*

3. *The land (Ps. 106:24; Jer. 3:19; Zech. 7:14).*

4. *Ships (Is. 2:16).*

5. *Plants (Is. 17:10).*

6. *Houses (Ezek. 26:12).*

7. *Vessels of silver and gold (Dan. 11:8).*

8. *Furniture (Nahum 2:9).*

The grammatical structure of this verse is most interesting. "Desire" is a *singular* subject and "shall come" is a *plural* verb! It literally reads, "the desire of all nations, they shall come." The "Desire of all nations" is the Messiah, the Lord Jesus Christ, our precious Savior. But the singular subject includes His Body in union with Him (1 Cor. 6:17; 1 Jn. 4:17). Together, Christ in the fullness of His Body, "they shall come." The plural predicate of Haggai 2:9 denotes His elect out of all nations, those whom God has from eternity foreknown and predestinated, and whom in time He calls, justifies, and glorifies (Rom. 8:29-30; 1 Pet. 1:2). Christ in and among all of us is the hope of glory (Col. 1:27). God's desire is for Christ to be fully formed in His people (Gal. 4:19). Global shaking will bring forth the divine expectation, a finished temple filled with His glory! The "desire of all nations" is the manifestation and unveiling of the Pattern Son in His sons.

Rom. 8:19, NIV

The creation waits in eager expectation for the sons of God to be revealed.

The subject in Haggai 2:7 is collective, denoting the whole number as a unit. The verb is perfect tense, describing the act of coming, which extends through the centuries as a completed act. The timeless God already sees them all, from first to last, as having come! The Book of Revelation, the unveiling of the slain Lamb, presents

His brethren as one new Man—"He that overcometh" (Rev. 2:26-27; 3:21; 21:7).

The shaking of Haggai 2:7 is the beginning of sorrows, the birth-pangs of the womb of the morning (Ps. 110:1-3; Mt. 24:8). These deliverers, an overcoming manchild company of sons, shall be caught up to the place of God's authority (Rev. 12:5). They shall "come" or "enter in" to that which is within the veil, having "come" to the full growth of His stature. Some feel that the plural verb "shall come" points to the precious things that the nations will bring into the Church, the "forces" or "wealth" of the Gentiles, exemplified by the eight areas mentioned above (Is. 60:5). There is truth in that interpretation; the Magi brought their gifts to the Christ child (Mt. 2:1-12), but the purer and consummate Messianic intent of the passage reveals Christ in the fullness of His Body. From earliest times, Christian interpreters and Jewish rabbis have referred this passage to Messiah's coming.

The Hebrew word for "and" in Haggai 2:7 denotes an intensifying consequence in light of what has been stated. For the word "house," see Haggai 1:2; for the explanation of "glory," compare Haggai 1:8 and 2:3. The shaking of all things brings the glory of the Lord! The word for "fill" in verse 7 means "to fill, fulfill, overflow, ordain, endow." God filled His house with glory in Exodus 40:34-35, First Kings 8:11, and Second Chronicles 5:14. He comes suddenly to His temple in Malachi 3:1. The Messiah, the King and Lord of glory, was the ultimate house filled with the glory of Jehovah's name and nature (Ps. 24:7-10; Is. 11:10; Jas. 2:1).

Jn. 1:14, NIV

The Word became flesh and made His dwelling among us. We have seen His glory, the glory of the One and Only....

The Silver and the Gold

Hag. 2:8, KJV

The silver is mine, and the gold is mine, saith the Lord of hosts.

Hag. 2:8-9, TLB

"The future splendor of this Temple will be greater than the splendor of the first one! For I have plenty of silver and gold to do it! And here I will give peace," says the Lord.

The Lord now takes up another matter that had disturbed the remnant—insufficient funds. In the days of Solomon, gold had been so plentiful that silver counted for little (1 Kings 10:21). The mighty Ruler of the universe had already moved the rulers of this world, Cyrus and Darius, to give liberally and lavishly for this purpose (Ezra 1:1-11; 6:1-12). The global aftershocks of God's quake shakes loose the silver and gold, releasing riches in two dimensions:

1. *The shaking of the earth—the nations and the denominations—transfers natural riches into His Church and Kingdom (Is. 60; Rev. 21–22).*

2. *The shaking of the heavens—the imaginations— converts the spiritual riches, the silver (redemption)*

> *and the gold (divine nature), into His Church and Kingdom (2 Cor. 10:3-6; 1 Pet. 1:5).*

Is. 60:5, NIV

> *...the wealth on the seas will be brought to you, to you the riches of the nations will come.*

First, *natural* resources are shaken loose (Deut. 8:18; Ps. 49:10). The natural riches of the nations and denominations will flow into His one holy Nation. The wealth of the sinner is laid up for the just (Prov. 13:22). The creativity of the Holy Ghost will produce an abundance. Jesus Christ is our heavenly Joseph; He is the Lord of the harvest. He is a mighty man of wealth (Gen. 41:37-46; Ruth 2:1; Phil. 4:19). Worldwide economic cataclysm will shake loose the "silver" and the "gold." That happened when Moses and the Israelites bankrupted Egypt and "borrowed" or "asked" their former captors for 400 years of back wages. These treasures were later used to build the tabernacle in the wilderness (Ex. 12:35-36; 38:24). Similarly, the edict of Cyrus had released funds to rebuild Zerubbabel's Temple. God's abundance is wealth to be redistributed or given away, assets to be stewarded; it is the means by which every nation is to be evangelized with the gospel of the Kingdom.

This first word in Haggai 1:8 is "silver (from its pale color); by implication, money; price, property." Next, the word for "gold" is an unused root meaning "to shimmer; gold, figuratively, something gold-colored (i.e. yellow), as oil, a clear sky." It is mentioned several times by Haggai's contemporary Zechariah (Zech. 4:2,12; 6:11;

13:9; 14:14). The earth is the Lord's and everything in it (Ps. 24:1; 50:10; Is. 60:13-17). He has opened an expense account for those whom He sends (Ezra 6:8). We are heirs together with the One who possesses heaven and earth (Gen. 14:22). As Owner, God can transfer His wealth from one to another whenever He wills. The opponents who had hoped to bring the building project to a halt were ordered to pay the temple costs from royal revenue in their own taxation district (Ezra 6:8-12). This financial provision probably arrived just after Haggai's daring claim that *Jehovah-Tsebaoth* owned all the wealth and would meet their need (2 Cor. 9:8)!

Ps. 2:8, KJV

Ask of Me, and I shall give thee the heathen for thine inheritance, and the uttermost parts of the earth for thy possession.

Job 23:10, KJV

But He knoweth the way that I take: when He hath tried me, I shall come forth as gold.

First the *natural* is addressed, then the *spiritual*. The shaking of the earth—the nations and denominations—releases natural riches. But the shaking of the heavens—the imaginations—looses the true riches of our inheritance. Haggai 2:1 underscored the remnant's celebration of the Feast of Tabernacles without a crop. Likewise, we have seen little—no real harvest of souls, no abundance of spiritual fruit, or demonstration of the nature of God.

This shaking in the heavenlies releases the "silver," the Bible symbol for redemption. Up till now, evangelism has consisted of fish changing tanks—bored, carnal transplants who want to be entertained by new spiritual baby-sitters. But the inhabitants of the nations and denominations will be redeemed and saved. Evangelism in the Feast of Pentecost is only the pledge of what will be seen in the reality of Tabernacles (see Acts 2:41,47; 4:4; 5:14; Rev. 7:9). The spiritual quake will also produce much "gold," the biblical symbol for the divine nature. The fulfillment of the last feast will gather the harvest of the Spirit's real fruit in His people (Gal. 5:22-23). The silver and the gold is the Lord's, shaken loose in the Day of the Lord!

The Greater Glory

Hag. 2:9, KJV

The glory of this latter house shall be greater than of the former, saith the Lord of hosts: and in this place will I give peace, saith the Lord of hosts.

Hag. 2:9, NIV

"The glory of this present house will be greater than the glory of the former house," says the Lord Almighty. "And in this place I will grant peace," declares the Lord Almighty.

Hag. 2:9, NKJ

The glory of this latter temple....

Hag. 2:9, JB

The new glory of this Temple is going to surpass the old....

Hag. 2:9, AMP

...in this place will I give peace and prosperity....

Before us now is the central verse, the root text for *unshakeable peace*. Note that it is the "glory," not the "house" (1:2), that is greater. Zerubbabel's temple was significantly plainer than Solomon's. For a full treatment of the word for "glory," see Haggai 1:8; 2:3. The Bible unfolds the increasing procession of glory from Adam in the garden to Abraham on the plains of Mamre, from Moses' tabernacle to Solomon's temple and then the second temple, from the Lord Jesus to the corporate fullness of His glorious Church. The principle is consistent; the glory of the latter house is always "greater."

But what is the "latter" house? This word means "hinder; generally, late or last; specifically (as facing the east) western." *Vine's* adds, "at the back; later, future." The Bible terms "latter" days or "last" days stand for the days of the Messiah, the New Testament era (Is. 2:2; Mic. 4:1; Acts 2:17). This "latter" glory is for the latter end, the last days, the generation to come (Ruth 3:10; Job 19:25; Ps. 102:18). The One who is the First and the Last will complete His purpose (Is. 41:4; 44:6). In the pattern of Moses' tabernacle (Ex. 25:40), there was an outer court, a holy place, and the Most Holy Place. The "latter" was "at the back" on the most "western" end. The glory of this inner sanctuary cannot be appreciated from a distance; one must enter in to behold the curtain of fine twined linen. Jesus, the true tabernacle, showed His innate splendor to Peter, James, and John on the Mount of Transfiguration.

The Lord has promised to fill His house with a "greater" glory. This word means "great (in any sense); hence, older." It comes from a root that means "to be large (in various senses, as in body, mind, estate, or honor)." It is used of extended dimension, number, power, and value (see Gen. 1:21; 12:2; 39:9; Deut. 4:37). In the Old Covenant, God's dwelling place was confined to one nation, the people of Israel. In the New Covenant, it includes members of every nation, kindred, tongue, and people (Rev. 14:6). The glory of the latter house is far greater. This word for "greater" in verse nine is the same as for "high" priest (Hag. 1:1,12,14; 2:2,4). The greater glory is the higher glory of the Most Holy Place and the "more excellent ministry" of Jesus Christ after the order of Melchisedec, the high priestly realm (Heb. 8:1-6). Compare this concept in the writings of Haggai's companion Zechariah (Zech. 3:1,8; 6:11).

The former glory is the former rain; the "latter" or "greater" glory is the latter rain. Historically, the former rain took place in the Book of Acts; the "latter rain" began to fall during the restoration of the Pentecostal revival (1900-1906), and it has continued through 1948-1956 to the present. Experientially, the former rain is explained in Acts 2:38 and First John 5:8; the latter rain, the greater or surpassing glory (2 Cor. 3:10), is revealed in Ephesians 4:13. In the former rain, Jesus Christ is the Alpha, the beginning; in the latter rain, He is the Omega, the end, the completion.

The Hebrew word for "former" in Haggai 2:9 is the same translated as "first" in Haggai 2:3. It means "first, in place, time or rank; beginning; chief." Its root means "head." The basic meaning of this word is "first" in a series. God's purposes are ever moving forward, an on-going incarnation. This word is particular to Isaiah (see Is. 41:22; 42:9; 46:9; 61:4; 65:17). The Scriptures promise an end-time outpouring of both the former and latter rains (Hos. 6:3; Joel 2:23).

In This Place Will I Give Peace

The Septuagint (translated by Charles Lee Brenton, Grand Rapids, MI: Zondervan Publishers House, 1978), the Greek Old Testament, renders Haggai 2:9, "...even peace of soul for a possession to every one that builds, to raise this temple." Then and now, "this place" is Jerusalem, which means "the habitation of peace." The New Testament Church is the heavenly Jerusalem (Gal. 4:21-31; Heb. 12:22-24), and Jesus Christ is the King of Salem, the King of Peace (Heb. 7:2). The Body of Christ is the habitation of peace by the Spirit; Jesus, its glorious Head, *is* our Peace (Eph. 2:14, 19-22).

In its strictest context, "this place" was the ruined condition of Zerubbabel's unfinished temple. Practically applied, it can refer to an individual, a family, a workplace, a school, a local church, a city, or a nation. In an expanded sense, "this place" will be the whole earth, the whole creation (Hab. 2:14). Some have lost hope that anything could be raised up out of this place. Only God can do it...only God will do it. He has torn and He will heal us. Ichabod will become Ishi (1 Sam. 4:21; Hos. 2:16). The glory will return.

Our sole motivation must be to identify with a true work of the Holy Ghost in our generation. Our view of "this place" must be reprogrammed. The word for "place" in verse nine means "a standing, a spot; a locality; also (figuratively) of a condition (of body or mind)." *Vine's* adds that the verbal root means "to arise, stand up, come about"; the verbal noun means "place, height, statute, standing." The Hebrew root means "to rise" and indicates the heavenly places of Ephesians 1:3 and 2:6. This New Testament "place" is the place of full stature (Eph. 4:13), the place of His overlook, His perspective from the heights of Zion (Acts 17:30; Phil. 3:20). The prophet Hosea called the same experience "the third day" (Hos. 6:1-2) and declared that God would "raise us up." This is the place that Jesus has gone to prepare through His intercession (Jn. 14:2). The word for "give" in Haggai 2:9 reveals that this is all by God's grace (Zech. 4:7). It means "to deliver, give, place, set up, lay, make, do." This is the rest or peace that is given (Mt. 11:28; Jn. 3:27; 14:27).

Haggai 2:9 declares our basic theme: The primary characteristic of the latter house of greater glory will be an unshakeable *peace*, unbreakable relationships, in the time of global shaking! The Hebrew word for "peace" in this key verse is *shalom* (Strong's #7965) and means "safe, (figuratively) well, happy, friendly; also welfare, health, prosperity, peace." It comes from the primitive root *shalam* (Strong's #7999) which means "to be safe (in mind, body or estate); figuratively, to be completed; by implication, to be friendly; by extension, to reciprocate; to be sound." *Vine's* adds that *shalom* means "peace, completeness, welfare, health." It also signifies "peace," indicative of a prosperous relationship between two or more parties. The adjective *shalem* means "complete; perfect." The Septuagint, the Greek Old Testament, includes the translations of *eirene* ("peace; welfare; health") and *soteria* ("deliverance; preservation; salvation").

Eph. 2:14-15, NIV

For He Himself is our peace, who has made the two one and has destroyed the barrier, the dividing wall of hostility,

by abolishing in His flesh the law with its commandments and regulations. His purpose was to create in Himself one new man out of the two, thus making peace.

God has spoken peace unto his people (Ps. 85:8). He has opened His mouth and spoken His Word. Jesus Christ, the Word of God, is the Reconciler, the Prince and King of Peace, the Recipient and Administrator of rest (Is. 9:6-7; Mic. 5:5; Col. 1:20; Heb. 7:2). Unshakeable peace, unbreakable relationships…a Kingdom and a covenant people with an undivided heart that cannot be moved. This is Father's house, an eternal habitation of living stones. We have been predestined to become an army of peacemakers, full-grown sons in the image of the Firstborn. Global shaking cannot disturb peace that abides. Till now, we have been unable to get free from hassles and undercurrents. All murmurings, complainings, and unresolved discord must be dealt with. With great inward urgency, we must allow God to resolve every dissonance and conflict till nothing offends us, to reconnect past relationships for the greater purpose of unshakeable peace! We must reconcile with one another until the air is clear and clean, free of offenses, violations, neglect, and procrastination.

The Feast of Tabernacles is often strategically centered in places of great struggle and spiritual warfare. God's army is made for the storm (Ps. 50:1-5). Pregnant with the fullness of God (Gal. 4:19), we can become irritable. Disagree, but don't be disagreeable. At times we have not been at ease with each other; this must be healed. If you have walked away from the work of the Lord, shift gears and turn. That is difficult if all you've seen or believed has been marked by discouragement. How do you view this house? Through your eyes, or His? Most of its appearance has been filtered through our own interpretation of His expectation.

Apologize. Bend. Make things right. Pray…then obey. The house of God must undergo a stability, strength, unity, and common covenantal bond that nothing can shake apart! Our hearts must be made whole again. Only God can do this. Get involved with something that only He can accomplish. It is time for *Him* to work. Refocus His purpose; you are going to need His house and your involvement in it. The Church will be the city of refuge and safety in the time of global seizures; the place of preservation will be the place of unbreakable relationships. Our connection to that house will protect us through indwelling, prevailing peace.

The greater glory for most men will be rediscovered in the rubble of their present situation, the current ruined state of things. Discouragement has taught us the wrong things about this place, robbing us of purpose and calling. Fatigue and the weariness of going week after week to a wrecked situation cannot be healed until we stop the preoccupation of building our own personal lives. Learn to be thankful, to appreciate this day, the set time He has chosen to build up Zion and appear in His glory, the day when He raises up *this place.* This is the house and people that He has foreordained, the place from which His glorious light shall be released worldwide.

Reconnect to the original deposit of God within you. Invest that treasure in others (2 Cor. 4:6-7). The place of greater glory is the house, the locale, the region where you are presently fellowshipping. It's not over the rainbow or in the next field; it's right in front of you (Ruth 2:8-9, 21-23). There's no place like home....

Think about it. There are more stable, strong, supportive relationships in "this place" than any other. Discouragement's aim is to beguile you away from that. The day of shaking has begun. You may not have enough time to be built into another house, to build meaningful relationships from the ground floor.

To balance this, the Lord is strategically placing some of His troops into new assignments with expanded commissions. God will ask some to advance into larger wineskins, to make positive, progressive transitions; but one should never change houses because he is discouraged with "this place." People change churches, pastors change churches, churches change pastors, men and women change marriage partners...that's not the answer! Many times after such a move, nothing really changes.

The problem is internal and spiritual, not external or geographical. Before you jump into those kinds of drastic maneuvers, deal with your own heart. Are you disconnected from being a contributor to the house of the Lord? Have you put your own assessment upon His anticipation? Have you tried to conform God to your image? Have you tried to create a Jesus who will accommodate your present way of thinking and living? Be honest.

Don't be afraid. God is still with you. He brought you out of Egypt by the blood of the Passover Lamb. If you will repent, He will finish that good work. Commit yourself and everything He has put into your life to His use in a greater way. He may involve you with people and places that are not attractive to your flesh, but you have a role to play in the rebuilding of His house. Let that calling flourish into useful influence. Don't be easily moved or impressed with all the superfluous hype—something less than the fruit of the Spirit. Roll up your sleeves and go back to work. Renew relationships. He will raise you up in the function and operation of His own choosing. In Jesus' name, loose the Potter to His own desire and design. Concede to His mighty hand. Let Him refire you (Jer. 18:1-6).

The latter house of greater glory is the many-membered Body of Christ. What a magnificent corporate calling! But this living temple is made up of individual stones, and each stone must make his calling and election sure. Each member must maintain a *personal* altar of devotion, serving the Lord with his whole heart.

Part Three

The Purity of Unshakeable Peace— The Whole Heart!

Chapter Seven

The Repair

"…and that which they offer there is unclean."

Hag. 2:10-14

Assured of *Jehovah-Tsebaoth's* strength and abiding presence, the remnant continued their work on the temple. They had reestablished the corporate altar in 535 B.C. Now, fifteen years later, God began to deal with *individuals*—every family and each man. He expected pure worship, nothing less than the whole measure of their heart's devotion. This necessity had precedent. Under the Levitical economy, God cleansed the nation's worship annually, sanctifying the golden altar of incense with blood on the Day of Atonement (Lev. 16). Centuries later, mighty Elijah took 850 false prophets to task on a lonely mountain in the eyes of all Israel (1 Kings 18). Before the fire fell and the glory came, the man of God *repaired* the altar and bathed it with water—a symbol of the "renewing" of the Holy Ghost (Tit. 3:5).

Haggai had begun to prophesy in the sixth month. His contemporary, Zechariah, launched his ministry eight weeks later with a challenging message, simple and to the point (Zech. 1:3-4). The remnant had heard the Lord's messenger in the Lord's message; initial vision had been restored. But they had not turned to God with their whole heart. By the ninth month, though His people had received a double prophetic witness, the rebirth of their full affection and its reward of immediate blessing was yet to be realized.

Haggai 2:10-14 sets forth Jehovah's corrective call to separation and *pure worship*. The faint aroma of sanctity coming from their altar was too feeble to pervade the secular atmosphere of their daily lives. The ruined skeleton of a partial temple was like a dead body decaying in Jerusalem, contaminating everything. Holiness is not contagious, but sin is. The holy flesh of their sacrifices could not impact their labors. Working on the temple did not sanctify the people; rather, their skepticism and delay had desecrated His holy place. God was weary with their hypocrisy. They honored Him with their lips and accustomed order, but their hearts were far from Him (Is. 1:10-20).

Ask Now the Priests

Hag. 2:10-11, KJV

In the four and twentieth day of the ninth month, in the second year of Darius, came the word of the Lord by Haggai the prophet, saying.

Thus saith the Lord of hosts; Ask now the priests concerning the law, saying.

Hag. 2:11, NIV

This is what the Lord Almighty says: "Ask the priests what the law says."

Hag. 2:10, TLB

In early December, in the second year of the reign of King Darius, this message came from the Lord through Haggai the prophet.

Hag. 2:11, Berkeley

...Ask now the priests for instruction concerning the law.

Hag. 2:11, JB

...Ask the priests for a decision on this question.

Haggai's third oracle addresses the priests, the keepers of the sanctuary and the law of Moses. Compare the date of verse 10 with Haggai 1:1,15; 2:1,20. Three months had passed since *Jehovah-Tsebaoth* had inaugurated Haggai's public ministry. One month had passed since He sent Zechariah to confirm the Word. The word for "ask" in verse 11 is a primitive root that means "to inquire; by implication, to request; to demand; consult." The priests, set apart by blood and oil, knew the divine procedure, the way of approaching God. Don't be afraid to ask (Zech. 10:1; Mt. 7:7; James 4:2). The prophet's request for an answer was urgent. For God to bring blessing, the hearts of the people needed to be reconditioned. Haggai wanted a reply "now," a Hebrew particle of incitement and entreaty used throughout the restoration prophets (see Hag. 2:2,15,18; Zech. 1:4; 3:8; 5:5; Mal. 1:8-9; 3:10).

The word for "priests" in verse 11 is *kohen* (Strong's #3548) and means "one officiating, a priest." It is translated in the King James Version as "chief ruler, priest, prince, principal officer." The primitive root *kahan* means "to mediate in religious services; to officiate as a priest; figuratively, to put on regalia." *Kohen* is found 741 times in the Old Testament; it is mentioned eight times in Haggai, six times in Zechariah, and three times in Malachi. More than one third of the references to the "priests" are found in the Pentateuch. The Book of Leviticus, with over 175 uses of this word, is called the "manual of the priests." A "priest" is an authorized minister of deity who officiates at the altar, performing sacrificial, ritualistic, and mediatorial duties; he represents the people before God. The priests, as teachers of righteousness, were to put a difference between the holy and profane (see Lev. 10:10-11; Deut. 33:10; Ezek. 44:23-24; Mal. 4:4). In the New Testament, we are called to be a kingdom of priests (Ex. 19:1-6; 1 Pet. 2:9).

Mal. 2:7, NIV

> *For the lips of a priest ought to preserve knowledge, and from his mouth men should seek instruction— because he is the messenger of the Lord Almighty.*

The word for "law" in Haggai 2:11 is *towrah* and means "a precept or statute, especially the Decalogue or Pentateuch." Its primitive root means "to flow as water (to rain); transitively, to lay or throw (especially to shoot an arrow); figuratively, to point out (as if by aiming the finger), to teach." *Vine's* adds that *towrah* means "law; direction; instruction;" it occurs 220 times in the Hebrew Old Testament. The prophets called Israel to return to the "instruction" of God (Is. 1:10). Jeremiah predicted the New Covenant, the internalization of the Decalogue; in that day, God's people would willingly obey Him by the inward code of a new nature (Jer. 31:31-34).

More Than a "Touch"

Hag. 2:12, KJV

If one bear holy flesh in the skirt of his garment, and with his skirt do touch bread, or pottage, or wine, or oil, or any meat, shall it be holy? And the priests answered and said, No.

Hag. 2:12, NIV

"If a person carries consecrated meat in the fold of his garment, and that fold touches some bread or stew, some wine, oil or other food, does it become consecrated?" The priests answered, "No."

Hag. 2:12, TLB

"If one of you is carrying a holy sacrifice in his robes, and happens to brush against some bread or wine or meat, will it too become holy?" "No," the priests replied. "Holiness does not pass to other things that way."

Hag. 2:12, AMP

...flesh that is holy [because it has been offered in sacrifice to God],....And the priests answered, No! [Holiness is not infectious.]

Holiness is not contagious, but sin is. Moral cleanness cannot be transmitted, but moral pollution can. A healthy man cannot communicate his strength to his sick child, but the ailing youngster can pass the disease to the father. The word "if" in this verse is a primitive article meaning "lo (as expressing surprise)!" Only the Holy Spirit can reveal the amazing principle set before us.

Haggai's inquiry regarded lifting up or carrying "holy flesh." The word for "holy" refers to sacred things consecrated or hallowed unto the Lord's use, things ceremonially or morally "clean." *Vine's* adds, "holy thing or sanctuary." Holy flesh became "holy" when set apart for sacrificial purposes (Ex. 29:34; Jer. 11:25). The flesh of the sin offering was even called "most holy" (Lev. 6:25).

The word for "flesh" in Haggai 2:12 means "flesh (from its freshness)" and comes from a root meaning "fresh; full, rosy, (figuratively) cheerful; to announce (glad news)." The latter is rendered in the King James Version as "messenger, preach, publish, shew forth, (bear, bring, carry, tell good) tidings." The messenger of God is to carry the gospel, the announcement of good news, in "holy flesh." This sanctified flesh was carried in the "skirt" of the priest. This word means "an edge or extremity; specifically (of a bird or army) a wing, (of a garment or bed-clothing) a flap, (of the earth) a quarter, (of a building) a pinnacle." There are many lessons here for those who bear good tidings. Their priestly skirt:

1. *Is tied to the mercy seat of God (Ex. 25:20).*

2. *Is blue, the color of heavenly things (Num. 15:38).*

3. *Is a place of trust (Ruth 2:12).*

4. *Can represent the anointing (Ruth 3:9; Ps. 133:2).*

5. *Is a place of safety (Ps. 17:8; 91:4).*

6. *Can represent God's covenant (Ezek. 16:8).*

7. *Is a place of influence (Zech. 8:23).*

8. *Is a place of healing (Mal. 4:2).*

The sacrifice would be carried in the wing, corner, or border of the priest's "garment," or "covering, clothing." This word is translated as "apparel, raiment, robe, vesture" in the King James Version. Garments represent an office or ministry (Zech. 3:1-5).

The seer now introduces another key principle. The Hebrew word for "touch" in Haggai 2:12 is *naga* (Strong's #5060) and means "to touch, lay the hand upon; by implication, to reach; violently, to strike or smite." Many of God's people only want a "touch" from the Lord or His ministers. From the front porch of their ceiled houses, they are content to reach out and touch the Lord while He passes by. Their God is external and distant, impersonal; to them, the indwelling Christ remains a mystery. Haggai's question in verse 12 has to do with the holy flesh touching the people's:

1. *Bread, or "food, grain, or fruit."*

2. *Pottage, or "something boiled, soup."*

3. *Wine (effervescent, or fermented).*

4. *Oil, or **grease** (the root means "to shine").*

5. *Meat, or anything "edible."*

These five areas illustrate the lives of those satisfied with just a "touch" from God's hand. They insist upon eating their own bread and wearing their own apparel. They allow themselves to be called Christians while privately interpreting the Word and establishing their own righteousness (Is. 4:1). Like worldly Esau, carnal Christians want blessings without responsibility; be careful, there's death in that pot (Gen. 25:29,34; 2 Kings 4:38-40). Spiritual minors mix new wine with old bottles (Lk. 5:37-39). Their anointing oil is stale, not fresh (Pa. 23:5; 92:10; 133:2). The light is going out in Eli's tent; the glory and anointing is about to depart (1 Sam. 3:1-4; Is. 10:27). "All" (the meaning for the word "any" in Haggai 2:12) meat has bred worms like yesterday's manna.

The sanctified offerings could not communicate their holiness. The Lamb of God was the fulfillment of every Old Testament oblation. The incarnate Word embodied "holy flesh;" Jesus was the true temple, the house of the Father. Occasionally brushing against His life will never impart His godliness. He wants more than just a touch from His Bride. She is to be flesh of His flesh, bone of His bone, a companion of like nature (Jn. 6:48-58; Eph. 5:30). He yearns for the undivided love of her whole heart. Every local church contains core group people and multitude people, the permanent building and its scaffolding. The twelve wanted to know the secrets of Jesus' Kingdom; the crowd wanted the loaves and fishes. True disciples want *Him*; the rest just want a *touch*. The coming days will call for more than fellowshipping with the back of someone's head for an hour on Sunday morning. We must seek out our bones, initiate and cultivate covenantal relationships.

The ark of the covenant within David's tabernacle typifies the sacred secret of "Christ in you" (Col. 1:27). God's glory, especially with regard to the fivefold ministry (Eph. 4:11), is housed in New Testament tents of "holy flesh." A detached encounter with an apostle or prophet won't change your life. You can't have real intimacy with a book or tape. Go beyond elementary Christianity, the laying on of somebody's hands (Heb. 6:1-2). Mingle your life with godly leaders in the unbroken covenant of mutual submission, open communication, and prophetic impartation. Desire more than a touch. Become one in Him (Jn. 17:21)!

The word for "touch" in Haggai 2:12 also means "to strike or smite." Religious spirits prefer the "touch" of anger—a God or preacher who loves to whip them. They thrive on legalism, satisfied to dance all night with a partner named reproof. These spiritual masochists only seem happy when God's Word is stepping on their toes. They love a good beating. The children born to such perversion are fear, condemnation, frustration, and anger. Will this arbitrary "touching" of the Lord or His ministers make one "holy"? The priests responded (or replied) with a resounding "No!" Is true biblical holiness based upon religious legalism and the spirit of fear? No! *Repair* the altar. Make a fresh dedication to serve God by serving His people. We need more than just a touch. Substantial relationships with the Lord and His servants accentuate the lives of true worshipers.

A Dead Body

Hag. 2:13, KJV

Then said Haggai, If one that is unclean by a dead body touch any of these, shall it be unclean? And the priests answered and said, It shall be unclean.

Hag. 2:13, NIV

Then Haggai said, "If a person defiled by contact with a dead body touches one of these things, does it become defiled?" "Yes," the priests replied, "it becomes defiled."

Hag. 2:13, TLB

Then Haggai asked, "But if someone touches a dead person, and so becomes ceremonially impure, and then brushes against something, does it become contaminated?" And the priests answered, "Yes."

Hag. 2:13, AMP

...And the priests answered, It shall be unclean. [Unholiness is infectious.]

Holiness is not contagious, but sin is. The prophet asked the priests a second question. Could the touch of a dead body make all these things "unclean"? This word means "foul, polluted, or contaminated." *Vine's* notes this uncleanness to be a state of being, and that the Septuagint translations are *akathartos* ("impure; unclean") and *miaino* ("stain; defile"). See Leviticus 5:2; 7:19-21; 10:10; 13:45; 22:4. The word for "body" in verse 13 is *nephesh,* the Hebrew word for "soul" (Num. 5:1-3; 9:6-10). Man's soul is his intellect, emotions, and will—what he thinks, feels, and wants. To be carnally minded is death; but to be spiritually minded is life and peace (Rom. 8:1-6).

The touch of Christ housed in holy flesh will not sanctify you, but the mere touch of the walking dead can kill! Bad company corrupts good character (Num. 19:13). Dead bodies that profane His temple come in many shapes and sizes. A dead "body" can be an individual or a religious system,—the range includes everything from AIDS to a legalistic preacher. Keep yourself pure, ever watchful of unequal yokes, garments spotted by the flesh (2 Cor. 6:14-7:1; Jude 23). Have nothing to do with the fruitless deeds of darkness, but rather expose them (Is. 52:11; Eph. 5:11; Tit. 1:15).

So Is This Nation

Hag. 2:14, KJV

Then answered Haggai, and said, So is this people, and so is this nation before Me, saith the Lord; and so is every work of their hands; and that which they offer there is unclean.

Hag. 2:14, NIV

Then Haggai said, "So it is with this people and this nation in My sight," declares the Lord. "Whatever they do and whatever they offer there is defiled."

Hag. 2:14, TLB

Haggai then made his meaning clear. "You people," he said (speaking for the Lord), "were contaminating your sacrifices by living with selfish attitudes and evil hearts—and not only your sacrifices, but everything else that you did as a 'service' to Me."

Hag. 2:14, Knox

...Here is a whole people, a whole race, the Lord says, that shews defiled under My scrutiny....

Haggai's application is clear. As long as the Lord's house remained incomplete and their worship half-hearted, Judah was tainted and unclean. The ruined temple, a witness to their long-standing sins of negligence, stood like a corpse in their midst, defiling everything. "So" or "rightly so" was the Jewish remnant, ascribed again as a heathen nation. The word for "people" is the same as Haggai 1:2 and can mean "relative." The Jews were of one mind; their corporate attitude needed an overhaul. The word for "nation" (Hag. 2:7) is the term usually applied to Gentiles (aliens and strangers) because of their lack of faith and love toward God (Eph. 2:11-12). So was Haggai's community, literally, "before His face." The prophet becomes even bolder. No sacrifice offered in disobedience could be acceptable (1 Sam. 15:22-23). Every bit or "all" of the remnant's "work" was defiled or "unclean" (Hag. 2:13). This word in verse 14 means "work, deed, labor, or behavior" and is translated as "labours" in Haggai 2:17.

The work of their "hands" was unwashed; this word can mean "monument, manhood, power, or rule." All service and ministry needed to be sanctified again (Eccles. 5:6).

In their lust to be seen, men have erected religious monuments and personal altars to themselves and their doctrine, demanding worship. These vanities will be knocked over in the Day of the Lord (Rev. 18:1-13). Until our personal altars are *repaired*, all that we "offer" is defiled. This word in Haggai 2:14 means "to approach or bring near; to come near." Man's way of entrance is the "way of Cain." Unholy men are fugitives and vagabonds, accountable to no one. These are spots at the feast who greedily feed themselves without fear. They are clouds without water, trees without fruit. They are wandering stars caught in the snare of their fleshly orbits (Jude 10-13).

The word "there" in verse 14 refers to the Altar of Burnt Offerings, the only site for legitimate sacrifice (Ezra 3:3; Heb. 13:10). The Brazen Altar finds its complete fulfillment in the cross of Jesus Christ, the only place where sin is washed away (Acts 4:12). *There* my burdened soul found liberty...at Calvary. The only right way to come near the Lord is by blood sacrifice. Jesus Christ is man's exclusive access to God, the only valid entry into the realm of Spirit (Jn. 10:1,7; 14:6). We have an altar—His cross. Draw near and be healed (Ps. 65:4; Ezek. 44:16).

Those who refuse to *repair* the altar offer the sacrifice of the wicked—impure worship (Prov. 15:8; 21:4; 21:27). Rend your heart and come before the Lord with honesty and integrity. Don't turn your ear from His Word (Prov. 28:9).

Many are deceived, swept along and carried by the corporate anointing. King Saul, out to murder David, happened upon the spiritual influence of the company of prophets. This demon-possessed man stripped off his clothes and prophesied all night under their charisma, then hurried on the next morning to kill David!

1 Sam. 19:24, KJV

...Wherefore they say, Is Saul also among the prophets?

That proverb has become the funeral dirge of more than one great leader (2 Sam. 1:27). You may feel God, see God, and hear God in the corporate gathering, but how about *your* heart? Is is right with Him?

Rebuild the personal altar in your life and family. Do your first works over again. Make a fresh commitment to God in wholehearted worship. From the day you humble yourself and begin to repent, God will bless you.

Chapter Eight

The Reward

"...from this day will I bless you."

Haggai 2:15-19

The prophet's questions and the priests' answers had made the point. Jehovah wanted Judah's whole heart. The personal devotion of Jerusalem's citizens turned back to the Lord and His covenant. Unshakeable peace is the place of undisturbed worship. When we move out of divine rest in any area of life, we take our heart with us. Worry is sin. Are you overly concerned about someone or something? The peace of God cannot rule an anxious spirit. He wants an undivided heart in pure worship, free from the spirit of fear. The end-time Church is to be a people of *purity*. As we are rejoined to our first love, He will *reward* us with immediate blessings. The prophet Zechariah confirmed Haggai's promise, describing the benefits of obedience (Zech. 8:11-15). God's people would be the head, not the tail. Their renewed devotion would break the drought.

Again, Haggai tells the remnant to "consider" (Hag. 1:5,7; 2:18) and bend their hearts back to God's Word. He recapitulates his first sermon (Hag. 1:1-11) and reminds them of former days (Hag. 2:15-19) in order to punctuate their change of heart, memorialized from "this day."

Hag. 2:15, KJV

And now, I pray you, consider from this day and upward, from before a stone was laid upon a stone in the temple of the Lord.

Hag 2:15, NIV

Now give careful thought to this from this day on— consider how things were before one stone was laid on another in the Lord's temple.

Hag. 2:15, Berkeley

And now, please call to mind days now past, before a stone had been laid....

"From this day and upward" is a Hebrew idiom capable of referencing backward as well as forward in time. Here, the word "upward" means "backward." God's messenger takes Judah back three months to the "day" or moment "before" the work on the second temple had begun again. From this day they were to look backward to the time when the work had initially ceased, and remember fifteen subsequent years of neglect.

Zerubbabel's temple, like Solomon's, was built with "stone" (1 Kings 5:17; 6:7; 1 Chron. 29:2). This Hebrew word is *eben* (Strong's #68) and means "to build; a stone." It comes from the primitive root *banah* (Strong's #1129), which means "to build." The noun form of the latter is *ben*, the Hebrew word for "son." As noted in Haggai 1:2, God's ultimate intention is to make for Himself a Son who would be a corporate house of living stones (Gen. 28:22; 1 Pet. 2:5). The temple for God's glory is fashioned and furnished with His own unalterable nature (Hag. 1:8). Jesus Christ is revealed as the rock of ages in the Book of Psalms (Ps. 61:2; 94:22; 95:1). Compare Genesis 49:24, Deuteronomy 32:15,18; Second Samuel 23:3, and Isaiah 8:14; 28:16. God is our rock, showing stability and permanency. His sanctuary is like its Owner, a place of steadfast peace and unbroken covenant. He has chosen to abide and walk with us; we can rest on that (Ex. 17:2; Job 5:23).

Jesus Christ is the headstone (Ps. 118:22), the One with the sevenfold or complete anointing, the fullness of the Spirit. Jesus is God, the One who sees and knows all things (see Is. 11:1-2; Zech. 3:9; 4:7; Rev. 5:6). But what is the meaning of these stones (Josh. 4:6)? The Spirit of truth is gathering the outcasts of Israel from every nation, reviving His work in the midst of the years (Neh. 4:2). This people has the law of God written in their hearts and constitute an altar of stones, healed and whole, the place of sacrifice (Ex. 24:12; Deut. 27:6-8). His end-time remnant has been made smooth in the brook of God, ready for the battle (1 Sam. 17:40). The Day of the Lord is the designated time when God will arise and show mercy. He will rebuild Zion's stones and appear in His glory. In that hour, we will take pleasure in His corporate work, and be glorified with Him (Ps. 102:13-16; Zech. 9:16).

Stone Upon Stone

The apostle declared the glorious Church to be a "great house" with many members (2 Tim. 2:20). Each of us has been placed into that Body by His predetermined counsel and sovereign will. This work is ongoing, stone upon stone. These stones are "laid" one upon another in Haggai 2:15. This word means "to put, place, set, fix," and demonstrates the principle of placement. First, God "sets" His chosen ministries within the Body; then, He "places" the members under their tutelage until the Father's purpose is consummated (1 Cor. 12:18,28; Gal. 4:1-2).

Furthermore, Ezra 6:4 declares that there were *three* rows of great stones in the temple's foundation. As noted, God's Word is formatted in an *excellent* or *threefold* manner (Prov. 22:20). The basic premise of this maxim is the tabernacle of Moses with its outer court, holy place, and Most Holy Place (Ex. 25:8,40). Those three realms parallel the Feasts of Passover, Pentecost, and Tabernacles (Deut. 16:16). The constituency of His house has a foundational understanding of these things, line upon line, stone upon stone (Is. 28:9-10).

The temple of the Lord is built stone upon stone. When finished, this house will be blameless, a place of purity and peace. Line upon line, God will redeem us completely: spirit, soul, and body (1 Thess. 5:23). Our salvation experience is progressively unfolding as well as being once and for all. We are growing in grace from strength to strength, faith to faith, glory to glory. Stone upon stone, generation upon generation, God is building the house of the ages, with every man in his own turn, rank, or season (1 Cor. 15:23). We serve God in our generation by entering into the labors of our predecessors (Jn. 4:38).

The prophet closes out verse 15 by his first mention of the *temple*. This word and concept was covered in depth in Chapter Two (Hag. 1:2). The New Testament Church is the *naos* or "inner sanctuary" of God. Corporately, the "temple" in Haggai's prophecy is Zion, a throne-room people; individually, it speaks of the Most Holy Place, the realm of spirit—the heart. As stated in Haggai 2:15, the remnant had once again "considered" the Lord. It had not always been that way (Job 34:27; Heb. 3:1).

Letting Things Slip

Divine things can "slip" (Heb. 2:1) or "flow by, carelessly pass (miss)." They can slowly drift away like a boat that has slipped its mooring. Backsliding is gradual, almost numbing. Men allow the *rhema*, the living Word, to rush by them. Without His direction, they inevitably stray into the meaningless spectrum of building their own houses. Israel's most notorious deliverer let things slip. The lesson to be learned from Samson's life is quite simple: the anointing that empowers also sanctifies. He fell asleep on the lap of the strange woman; his anointing was gradually dismantled until the glory departed. The saddest part of the story is that he did not realize his deteriorating condition. Israel's mightiest judge was left blind, bound, and going in circles (Judg. 16:20-21).

The prophet Haggai now indicates the remnant's progressive decline. Those content with a partial inheritance are under a curse, but they do not know it (Lev. 26:20; Deut. 28:16; Mal. 2:2). Haggai 2:15 emphasizes God's house being constructed stone upon stone; verse 16 shows reverses the principle.

Hag. 2:16, KJV

Since those days were, when one came to an heap of twenty measures, there were but ten: when one came to the pressfat for to draw out fifty vessels out of the press, there were but twenty.

Hag. 2:16, NIV

When anyone came to a heap of twenty measures, there were only ten. When anyone went to a wine vat to draw fifty measures, there were only twenty.

Hag. 2:16, TLB

Before, when you expected a twenty-bushel crop, there were only ten. When you came to draw fifty gallons from the olive press, there were only twenty.

Hag. 2:16, AMP

Through all that time [the harvests have not fulfilled expectations]....

"Since those days were" recollects the years 535-520 B.C. when the remnant was remiss in its duty. The Amplified Bible renders it, "Through all that time..." Haggai observed that things had gone from bad to worse since their efforts had been deferred (Ezra 4:24). The Septuagint expresses the question of verse 16, "How did you fare?"

The word for "heap" reflects the harvest and means "a heap; a sheaf"; it comes from a root meaning "to pile up" and is translated in the King James Version as "gather together." The Lord's intention is to reap a mighty harvest, a heap of corn (Ruth 3:7; Song 7:2). The consecrated tithe, the abundance of the Lord, is to be a mountain of blessing with plenty for the priests and people (2 Chron. 31:6-7). The word for "twenty" in Haggai 2:16 comes from a primitive root that means "to accumulate; to grow, (make) rich." It restates the Father's desire to gather and favor His children. The remnant had continued to celebrate the Feast of Ingathering without a harvest. They had sown and looked for much, but brought in little (Hag. 1:6,9).

First, they had expected "twenty" measures of corn, but only realized "ten," or 50 percent. Corn symbolizes the Word of God. Fifty, half of one hundred, is the number for Pentecost. The Pentecostal experience is the firstfruits and earnest and pledge of our destiny (Rom. 8:23; Eph. 1:13-14). Though we publish Tabernacles, we have only experienced two feasts. We may preach a hundredfold message, but the "word made flesh," in the way we live and through the fruit we manifest, is still sixtyfold…in part. Second, Haggai's congregation had gone to the winepress looking for "fifty" measures, but only drew out "twenty," or 40 percent. Thus is revealed the gradual decline, from 50 to 40 percent. Wine symbolizes the outpoured joy of the Holy Ghost. The anointed purpose of God was slipping away, little by little. Many Pentecostals have retreated back to the outer court in the name of academics and sacramental liturgy (Is. 5:2). Limited vision will eventually fail; it cannot feed the inner man (Is. 63:3; Hos. 9:2). This spiritual lapse is subtle, almost imperceptible, until men lose their sensitivity (Eph. 4:19).

The word for "pressvat" in Haggai 2:16 is from an unused root meaning "to excavate; a trough (as dug out); specifically, a wine-vat (whether the lower one, into which the juice drains; or the upper, in which the grapes are crushed)." The word for "draw" means "to drain away or bail up a liquid." We are drawn to the Lord in order to draw from the Lord (Song 1:4; Jn. 4:11-15). The word for "press" in this verse means "a winepress (as crushing the grapes)." The Bible declares that the "winepress," the constant flow of the Holy Spirit in our lives and churches:

1. *Is to be full, ever increasing (Num. 18:27,30).*

2. *Is to be a blessing to others (Deut. 15:14).*

3. *Is to be the place where the enemy is slain (Judg. 7:25).*

4. *Is to be a place of shouting (Is. 16:10; Jer. 48:33).*

5. *Is to be the place of overflowing life (Joel 2:24; 3:13).*

6. *Is to be the property of the King (Zech. 14:10).*

We have entered a season where everything is intensifying and accelerating. Now is not the time to hold back. The *purity* of unshakeable peace is that we renew our personal altars, giving our whole heart to the Lord. The *reward* of immediate blessings will follow (Prov. 3:9-10).

Blasting, Mildew, and Hail

Hag. 2:17, KJV

I smote you with blasting and with mildew and with hail in all the labours of your hands; yet ye turned not to Me, saith the Lord.

Hag. 2:17, NIV

"I struck all the work of your hands with blight, mildew and hail, yet you did not turn to Me," declares the Lord.

Hag. 2:17, NEB

I blasted you and all your harvest with black blight and red and with hail, and yet you had no mind to return to Me, says the Lord.

The remnant's disregard for God's House had brought righteous judgment (Hag. 1:11). The word for "smote" here means "to strike" and is rendered in the King James Version as "beat, kill, punish, slaughter, wound." Consider Psalms 3:7; 50:6; 53:4. See also Malachi 4:6 and its prominent usage in the Book of Zechariah (Zech. 9:4; 10:11; 12:4; 13:6-7). God had "smitten" Pharaoh, Amalek, and the Philistine giant (Ex. 3:20; 1 Sam. 15:3; 17:49). Because of their stubbornness, He had become the adversary of His own people (Is. 63:10)!

Deut. 28:22, NIV

The Lord will strike you with wasting disease, with fever and inflammation, with scorching heat and drought, with blight and mildew, which will plague you until you perish.

The word for "blasting" in Haggai 2:17 means "blight" and comes from a primitive root that means "to scorch." God had "blasted" the corn before it grew up (2 Kings 19:26). The word for "mildew" means "paleness, whether of persons (from fright), or of plants (from drought); in the sense of vacuity of color; pallor, the yellowish green of young and sickly vegetation." Interestingly, it comes from a root that means "to spit," signifying uncleanness and defilement (Lev. 15:8; 18:28; 20:22). The One who carried our griefs and sorrows at Calvary was also the recipient of our spit (Is. 53:3-4; Mt. 26:67; Mk. 10:34).

The returning Jews were like sickly plants needing to be healed. They had exchanged truth for lies, God's vision for their own (Rom. 1:23-25). Mildew, the spit of His judgment, was the repercussion of easy living in the demilitarized zone, not committed to either kingdom (Rev. 3:16). Blasting, mildew, and "hail" is symbolic for judgment throughout the Old Testament (Ex. 9:18), especially in the Book of Psalms (Ps. 78:47; 105:32; 148:8) and the Book of Isaiah (Is. 28:2; 30:30; 32:19). Compare Joshua 10:11; Ezekiel 13:11-13; 38:22 with Revelation 8:7; 11:19; 16:21.

The Mark of the Beast

The mark of the beast is a present reality. This principle of present truth was discussed at length in Chapter Seven of my book *The More Excellent Ministry*. In summary of this principle, the Greek word for "mark" in Revelation 13:13-18 is *charagma* and means "a mark, stamp, or impress." The word for "beast" is *therion*, and it means "a wild beast," the nature of unregenerate man. The old man is a brute; Adam's paw print, the impression of human wisdom and strength, is revealed in the forehead and right hand. The carnal works of Haggai's community were judged by the Lord of hosts (Hag. 1:11;

2:14,17). The remnant in Haggai's day had exchanged God's original vision for merely a good idea. Corporate business and religious organizations are built with man's notions and man's money to back them. Human cleverness comes from the tree of death, divine wisdom from the Tree of life. Every witty invention and vain imagination will be shaken and judged in the Day of the Lord (Hag. 2:7).

The mark and seal of the Lord is altogether different (Hag. 2:23). Christ is the wisdom and power of God (1 Cor. 1:24). Father God has a dream house! What His mind has conceived, His "hand" will fashion according to His original design and image (1 Cor. 3:10; Eph. 4:11). A Word from God must always precede a work for God (Hag. 1:12-13). Every project not sanctioned by His will must be judged and put to an open shame (Ps. 78:46; Jer. 3:24). Every house assembled without His authorization will be burned with fire.

"...yet ye turned not to Me" (Amos 4:9). Before Haggai's and Zechariah's reprimand, the remnant had not willingly "considered" (Hag. 1:5) or "turned" back to God's purpose (Job 36:13; Is. 9:13; Rev. 2:21). They had stubbornly refused the work for which the Lord had first called them. The word of His prophets is necessary. Otherwise, men will remain content with only half their spiritual potential, refusing to repent (Jer. 5:3).

From the Foundation

Hag. 2:18, KJV

Consider now from this day and upward, from the four and twentieth day of the ninth month, even from the day that the foundation of the Lord's temple was laid, consider it.

Hag. 2:18, NIV

From this day on, from this twenty-fourth day of the ninth month, give careful thought to the day when the foundation of the Lord's temple was laid. Give careful thought.

Hag. 2:18, ASV

Consider, I pray you, from this day and backward, from the four and twentieth day of the ninth (month), since the day that the foundation of Jehovah's temple was laid, consider it.

Following this statement, the prophet begins to announce the promised *reward* of Jehovah's immediate blessings. Haggai takes us back to the time when Zerubbabel and his company laid the temple's foundation (Ezra 3:6-11). From "this day" in this verse is defined as the 24th day of the ninth month, the day Haggai spoke this message. The word "upward" is again "backward" (Hag. 2:15). From "this day" they were to consider backward to the moment when the foundation of the sanctuary was laid.

For the word "consider," see Haggai 1:5,7; 2:15. Used five times in this book, it reveals the principle of grace. Only God can empower us to set our hearts back on the primary vision. The word for "foundation" means "to set; to found; to sit down together, to settle, consult," and it is also translated as "appoint, take counsel, establish, instruct, lay, ordain" in the King James Version. This word is used in First Kings 5:17, Job 38:4, Psalms 24:2; 102:25, and Amos 9:6; it is most prominently used in the Book of Isaiah (see Is. 14:32; 28:16; 44:28; 51:16; 54:11). Compare this to Zechariah 8:9. The consistent theme and message of Haggai is that the house of the Lord is to be built and finished. In this ancient Messianic prophecy, the Lord Jesus is portrayed as:

1. *The Father's house and temple (Col. 1:19; 2:9).*

2. *The altar of burnt offerings (Heb. 13:10).*

3. *The sure foundation (1 Cor. 3:11).*

Ps. 24:7-8, KJV

Lift up your heads, O ye gates; and be ye lift up, ye everlasting doors; and the King of glory shall come in.

Who is this King of glory? The Lord strong and mighty, the Lord mighty in battle.

Psalms 22, 23, and 24 hail Jesus Christ as mankind's Savior, Shepherd, and Sovereign; the latter is His coronation song. The Jewish remnant returned, built the altar, and laid the foundation to Zerubbabel's temple. Two thousand years ago, Jesus Christ defeated sin and satan, passed through the heavenlies and ascended His throne (Col. 2:15; Heb. 4:14-16; Rev. 3:21). The Word forever settled in heaven is humanity's new altar and sure foundation! Since His exaltation, the real purpose and work of God has been postponed, not for fifteen years, but two millennia! The Dark Ages have come and gone. Though the Protestant Reformation began to restore the years (Joel 2:25), His house is still not finished. The Church, which is His Body, is still immature and incomplete. Who is there among you who will hear His prophet and revive the divine scheme, the holy enterprise? Let Him go up to the mountain and bring wood. Let him build and become the habitation of unshakeable peace and glory.

Seed in the Barn

Haggai was a brave preacher. The seed was in the soil, not the barn. In the middle of winter, no one would have dared to forecast the quality of next year's harvest...no one except a real prophet. The harvest had failed. Up till now, the seed had been consumed or used for sowing. But the prophet's words had convinced the remnant to bring their offerings back into God's House. Haggai's congregation had repaired the altar and repositioned their hearts; they were about to inherit the *reward* of immediate gain (2 Chron. 31:10).

Hag. 2:19, KJV

Is the seed yet in the barn? yea, as yet the vine, and the fig tree, and the pomegranate, and the olive tree, hath not brought forth: from this day will I bless you.

Hag. 2:19, NIV

Is there yet any seed left in the barn? Until now, the vine and the fig tree, the pomegranate and the olive tree have not borne fruit. "From this day on I will bless you."

Hag. 2:19, TLB

Notice, I am giving you this promise now....

The word for "seed" in this verse means "seed; figuratively, fruit, plant, sowing-time, seedtime, harvest, offspring, descendants, posterity." It comes from a primitive root meaning "to sow; figuratively, to disseminate, plant, fructify." It is mentioned over 200 times in the Old Testament, especially in:

1. *The Book of Genesis (see Gen. 1:11-12; 3:15; 15:5; 22:17).*

2. *The Book of Psalms (see Ps. 18:50; 22:30; 25:13; 37:25; 126:6).*

3. *The Book of Isaiah (see Is. 6:13; 53:10; 54:3; 61:9).*

Seedtime is harvesttime. Haggai's whole prophecy anticipates a global ingathering. There can be no harvest while the seed is "yet in the barn." The American Church must repent. Ninety-five percent of the ministries have laid up corn in but five percent of His Body; still the seed lies spoiled. We must look again to our Example. Jesus Christ is the Seed that left the "barn"—the bosom of the Father—and was planted in the earth (Jn. 1:1-4,14). This word means "a granary; a place of lodging; an abode or residence." He is that Bread of life (Jn. 6:48). The Messiah was the Seed of the woman, the Seed of Abraham, and the Seed of David. Thus is revealed His pain, promise, and power as He relates to all men racially, redemptively, and royally. The Bible is the story of the Word, the Seed:

1. *The Seed comes—Genesis to Malachi (Gen. 3:15).*

2. *The Seed dies—Matthew to John (Jn. 12:24).*

3. *The Seed lives—the Book of Acts (Acts 2:24).*

4. *The Seed speaks—Romans to Jude (Heb. 1:1).*

5. *The Seed reigns—the Book of Revelation (Rev. 11:15).*

The Feast of Tabernacles is a street revival. The members of the Church, the seed of the Kingdom, must leave their comfortable pews and lofty stain-glassed windows to minister resurrection life to the common man. The message of Tabernacles has been preached for almost fifty years, but men have imprisoned its seed within self-serving agendas. The Body of Christ lies waste while we build bigger barns for unused seed. Our treasure, our hearts, are misplaced (Lk. 12:15-21). We have proclaimed the right declaration—Jesus Christ is Lord of all (Rev. 19:16)—in the wrong location! This absolute truth must be declared in the heavenlies as a witness to principalities and powers (Eph. 3:10) by means of prophetic worship and intercession. It must be preached in the darkest corners of the earth (Ps. 2:8) by means of Kingdom evangelism. Believers have been commanded and commissioned to replicate His word and ministry of reconciliation (2 Cor. 5:17-21), not just to prophesy to each other.

This imaging is "yet" to take place. This word in Haggai 2:19 means "iteration or continuance; again, repeatedly, still, more." It comes from a primitive root that means "to duplicate or repeat; to protest, testify (as by reiteration); intensively, to encompass, to restore (as a sort of reduplication)." Jesus Christ shall see His Seed, the travail of His soul; the Church will prolong His days (Is. 53:10-11; Jn. 17:20-24; Acts 1:1). A people conformed to His image was the joy set before our Lord (Rom. 8:29; Heb. 12:1-3). The Father glorified His name in Jesus

Christ; He will do it *again* in the house of enduring peace
(Jn. 12:28). As mature ambassadors of the New Covenant,
His sons have been apprehended to reproduce His name
and nature.

The Vine, Fig, Pomegranate, and Olive

Hag. 2:19, KJV

> *...the vine, and the fig tree, and the pomegranate,*
> *and the olive tree, hath not brought forth....*

Until now, Jehovah's vine, like Jerusalem's unfinished
temple, has lain waste (Joel 1:7,12; Hab. 3:17). The restored Church, the Body of Christ, the house of the Lord,
is designated by the prophet to be the Lord's:

1. *Vine.*

2. *Fig tree.*

3. *Pomegranate.*

4. *Olive tree.*

First, the restored Church is His vine. The Hebrew
word for "vine" in Haggai 2:19 is *gephen* (Strong's #1612)
and means "to bend; a vine (as twining), especially the
grape." It is translated in the King James Version as "vine,
tree." First mentioned in Noah's time (Gen. 9:20-21), the
vine was celebrated for its luxurious growth and immense clusters. The grapes were gathered with shouts of
joy, put into baskets, and carried to the winepress. Jesus
Christ is the true or genuine Vine (Jn. 15:1-7). The new
wine is found in the cluster of His Body (Is. 65:8). This
restates Haggai's theme of corporate vision, to rebuild

the whole house of the Lord—His Church, to be in union with Him:

1. *Is bound to the Lord in choice covenant (Gen. 49:11).*

2. *Is delivered from Egypt—the world (Ps. 80:8,14).*

3. *Is marked by the fragrance of worship (Song 2:13).*

4. *Is known as the place of refuge and safety (Zech. 3:10).*

5. *Is destined to bear full grown fruit (Mal. 3:11).*

Zech. 8:12, KJV

> *For the seed shall be prosperous; the vine shall give her fruit....*

Second, the restored Church is His fig tree. The word for "fig tree" in verse 19 is *te'en* (Strong's #8384) and means "the fig (tree or fruit)." The fig, a pear-shaped fruit, was much used for food, prized for its sweetness and flavor. An emblem for God's holy nation, its blossoms appear before the leaves. Until we participate in the vision of completing His House, our figs will fall from the tree (Ps. 105:33; Is. 34:4; Jer. 8:13). We must be transformed from being "naughty figs" to His "first ripe" figs, His firstfruits company in the earth (see Jer. 24:1-8; 29:17; Nahum 3:17; Zech. 3:10).

Mic. 4:4, KJV

> *But they shall sit every man under his vine and under his fig tree; and none shall make them afraid: for the mouth of the Lord of hosts hath spoken it.*

Third, the restored Church is His pomegranate. The word for "pomegranate" in Haggai 2:19 is *rimmown* (Strong's #7416) and means "a pomegranate, the tree (from its upright growth) or the fruit (also an artificial ornament)." It comes from a primitive root that means "to rise," translated in the King James Version as "exalt, get up, lift up, mount up." The pomegranate is a tall bush rather than a tree. Its foliage is dark green with crimson flowers; its fruit is red when ripe, containing a quantity of juice. God's remnant are the upright, the righteous, filled with His life and rising up to serve His purpose. As the pomegranate, we are:

1. *Priests marked by the fruit of the Spirit (Ex. 28:33-34).*

2. *The firstfruits of His land (Num. 13:23; Deut. 8:8).*

3. *A resting place for kings (1 Sam. 4:12).*

4. *Ornaments which beautify His temple (1 Kings 7:20).*

5. *Those who have the mind of Christ (Song 4:3).*

6. *The people of His pleasure (Song 4:13; 6:11).*

7. *Those who drink the wine of His Kingdom (Song 8:2).*

Song 7:12, KJV

Let us get up early to the vineyards; let us see if the vine flourish, whether the tender grape appear, and the pomegranates bud forth: there will I give thee my loves.

Fourth, the restored Church is His olive tree. The word for "olive" in verse 19 is *zayith* (Strong's #2132) and means "an olive (as yielding illuminating oil), the tree, the branch or the berry." It comes from a root meaning "to be prominent; properly, brightness; (figuratively) the month of flowers; Ziv." Compare the principles concerning Mount Olivet found in Haggai 1:8. The olive was abundantly characteristic of Judah; almost every village had its own grove. The cultivation of the olive tree had the closest connection with Judah's domestic life, trade, and public worship. This tree thrives best in warm and sunny situations, growing slowly and living to an immense age. Emblematic of God's people, the olive tree provides a picture of vigor, strength, and prosperity.

To make the olive oil, the fruit was either bruised in a mortar, crushed in a press loaded with wood or stones, ground in a mill, or trodden with the feet. The oil was used as food, a cosmetic for anointing the body after a bath, a medicine, or for fueling the temple lights. It was mixed with the flour or meal used in offerings. Kings and priests were anointed with oil, and the Jew was required to include oil among his tithe and firstfruits offerings. The berry of the olive tree was pressed to yield illuminating oil, a symbol for the Holy Spirit. The remnant Church is a Spirit-filled people of prayer and praise. We have gone to Gethsemane, which means "olive-press." Those who have surrendered to do the will of the Father are:

1. *Messengers of peace and good news (Gen. 8:11).*

2. *Anointed according to divine pattern (Ex. 30:24).*

3. *Living ones who trust the Lord (Ps. 52:8).*

4. *The children at His table (Ps. 128:3).*

5. *A people of beauty and glory (Hos. 14:6).*

6. *Sons of oil (Zech. 4:3).*

What a glorious calling! The rebuilt temple, the restored house of the Lord, has been promised a "good land."

Deut. 8:7-8, NIV

For the Lord your God is bringing you into a good land—a land with streams and pools of water, with springs flowing in the valleys and hills;

a land with wheat and barley, vines and fig trees, pomegranates, olive oil....

From This Day Will I Bless You

Jehovah had foreordained this providence for His people. He is a faithful God, willing to forgive. Haggai's prophecy, like a legal document, was dated. From "this day," the twenty-fourth day of the ninth month, 520 B.C., God would bless Judah! The word for "brought forth" (Hag. 2:19) means "to lift or raise up; remove, depart, carry away." God's Church will be brought from the barn and raised up to live in His sight, partakers of resurrection life (Hos. 6:1-2). The same Spirit that raised Jesus Christ from the dead now quickens a people for His name (Rom. 8:11). Like John, we have been carried away in Spirit to behold the Bride, the Lamb's wife (Rev. 21:9-11). The remnant had repaired the altar and offered the Lord their whole heart that His house might be completed. Judah had been restored as His vine and pomegranate, His fig and olive trees. Jehovah now gives obedience's benediction (Mt. 6:33).

The word for "bless" in verse 19 means "to kneel; to bless God (as an act of adoration) and man (as a benefit)." The remnant knelt before their Maker, realigned to receive His word and will (Gen. 1:28; 12:3; 22:17). Haggai's word had changed their heart. The manifest presence of the Lord was with His people. He had turned to show them pity and mercy (Joel 2:14), and would fill His house with glory and peace (2 Sam. 6:11; Ps. 29:11). From the day we give Him our whole heart, He will bless us (Deut. 15:10; Ps. 133:3).

Mal. 3:10, NIV

...I will...throw open the floodgates of heaven and pour out so much blessing that you will not have room enough for it.

The altar's *repair* had produced obedience's *reward*. The *purity* of unshakeable peace is expressed in wholehearted devotion to the Lord. At His feet lay dismantled thrones and every other crown. Pure worshipers who allow Him to fully cleanse His temple will be given the right to share His authority and wear His ring.

The Lord is coming to America and the nations with a scourge of small cords in His hand (Jn. 2:15). In the day of overturning, He will *remove* out of His Kingdom all things that offend. The Head of the house, the Lord of the harvest, the Host of the Feast, is about to tip the tables again.

Part Four

The Prince of Unshakeable Peace— The Whole Dominion!

Chapter Nine

The Removal

"And I will overthrow the throne of kingdoms..."

Haggai 2:20-22

On the twenth-fourth day of the seventh month, Haggai received a public word for the whole remnant (Hag. 2:10); the same day, he heard this specific promise for Zerubbabel, governor of Judah (Hag. 1:1; 2:21; Ezra 5:2).

The *purpose* of unshakeable peace is to complete the temple—to save the whole man. God's abode, His eternal house in the heavens, is the Body of Christ. The complete outworking of Jesus' death, burial, and resurrection will be the full redemption of our spirit, soul, and body (1 Thess. 5:23). How big is the Father's plan of restoration? The *parameter* of unshakeable peace is the whole earth. All creation and every area of our lives will be impacted and leavened by His Spirit. Heaven and earth will yield up a Kingdom that cannot be moved (Heb. 12:25-29). What does the Creator want from His creation? The *purity* of unshakeable peace is the whole heart given to the Lord in pure worship. We yearn for more than a "touch" from God. We are called to be bone of His bone, flesh of His flesh..."holy flesh" (Eph. 5:30-32).

But what is the ground of assurance that the Father will perform this glorious Word? The prophetic crescendo climaxes. Haggai's final utterance spotlights the surety and guarantee of this New Covenant—the *prince* of unshakeable peace, the Lord Jesus Christ, the One to whom is given the whole dominion! This living hope is the seedbed of real faith. Jesus alone has the covenantal jurisdiction to overthrow the kingdoms of our heart (Hag. 2:20-22). He is heir of all things (Heb. 1:2), including all authority, prefigured by the "signet" of Haggai 2:23. Worship is the basis of His government. Those who give Him their whole heart will ascribe to His dominion. Under the Levitical economy, the heart of the sacrifice constituted the wave offering; the animal's shoulder was thrown on the altar in the heave offering. When God has a man's heart, He has his shoulder, the place of responsibility (Prov. 21:1; Is. 9:6).

A Personal Shaking

Hag. 2:20-21, KJV

> *And again the word of the Lord came unto Haggai in the four and twentieth day of the month, saying,*
>
> *Speak to Zerubbabel, governor of Judah, saying, I will shake the heavens and the earth.*

Hag. 2:20, NIV

> *The word of the LORD came to Haggai a second time on the twenty-fourth day of the month.*

Hag. 2:20-21, TLB

Another message came to Haggai from the Lord that same day:

Tell Zerubbabel, the governor of Judah, "I am about to shake the heavens and the earth."

Hag. 2:21, Knox

...Earth and heaven both I mean to set rocking....

In Haggai 1:1; 2:1,10, the word of the Lord came "by the hand of" Haggai. Here in verse 20, the word of the Lord comes "unto" or "to" the prophet. The remnant had rebuilt the national altar of burnt offerings, then restored the personal altar—the individual heart (Hag. 2:10-14). So the *corporate* upheaval of Haggai 2:6-9 parallels the *individual* shaking given in verse 21. For the meaning of this "shaking" of the heavens and the earth, see Haggai 2:6. The principles and truths about this personal upheaval complements those set forth in the exegesis of Haggai 2:7,22. The purpose of this particular shaking is to prepare the individual house for His glory. Every valley shall be exalted, and every mountain and hill made low (Is. 40:3-5; Zech. 4:7). All that remains is a permanent Kingdom of never-failing peace (Mt. 7:24-27).

The Triple Overthrowing

Judah was small and defenseless, but the Lord said, "I will overthrow..." (Hag. 2:27). God will rise to the prey. We will not have to fight in this battle. He works all things together to perform His Word and will.

Hag. 2:22, KJV

And I will overthrow the throne of kingdoms, and I will destroy the strength of the kingdoms of the heathen; and I will overthrow the chariots, and those that ride in them; and the horses and their riders shall come down, every one by the sword of his brother.

Hag. 2:22, NIV

I will overturn royal thrones and shatter the power of the foreign kingdoms. I will overthrow chariots and their drivers....

Hag. 2:22, TLB

...I will overthrow their armed might....

Hag. 2:22, NKJ

...I will destroy the strength of the Gentile kingdoms....

Hag. 2:22, Knox

...royal thrones shall be overturned, and the power of Gentile kingdoms brought to nothing; overthrown they lie...down come horse and rider....

This verse amplifies Haggai 2:7. As noted earlier, God's plan and purpose is formatted in threes (Prov. 22:20). God's purpose disclosed in Haggai 2:22 includes a triple or threefold overthrowing:

1. *"I will overthrow the throne of kingdoms."*

2. *"I will destroy the strength of the kingdoms of the heathen."*

3. *"I will overthrow the chariots and those that ride in them."*

Ezek. 21:27, KJV

I will overturn, overturn, overturn, it: and it shall be no more, until He come whose right it is; and I will give it Him.

This prophecy to King Zedekiah of Judah emphasizes the end of lawlessness; the thrice-mentioned word for "overturn" is unique to its context. All ungodly authority will be dealt with—"overthrown" and removed. Messiah alone would bear rule in the earth, the exalted One to whom it rightfully belongs. For Jesus Christ to be Lord of all, every Christian experiences a personal overturning in each realm of his threefold growth in grace (Prov. 22:20):

Outer Court	Holy Place	Most Holy Place
Passover	Pentecost	Tabernacles
Out of Egypt	Through the desert	Into the land
Born again	Spirit-filled	Mature
Baptism in water	Baptism in Spirit	Baptism in fire
Babes	Youth	Men
All man	God and man	All God

When God first delivered us from sin and placed us in His family, He turned our world upside down. The new birth was the beginning of our salvation, and the subsequent Pentecostal experience soon became our birthright. When Jesus baptized us with the Holy Ghost with the evidence of speaking in other tongues, He overthrew the traditions of men a second time. The Body of Christ has experienced two overturnings: Passover and Pentecost. We stand at the threshold of the third. Once again, Jesus is sending apostles and prophets to create havoc among the complacent (Lk. 11:49). Doctor Luke, describing apostolic ministry in the early Church of Acts, provides great insight into this current spiritual upheaval.

Acts 17:6, KJV

...These that have turned the world upside down are come hither also.

The Greek word for "turned upside down" is *anastatoo* (Strong's #387) and it means "removal; drive out of home; disturb." The word for "world" is *oikoumene* (*oikos* is the Greek word for "house"). Paul and the apostolic company had torn up the religious house of Judaism on their way to Athens. They were about to disturb the Greeks, the "college crowd," as well. All men seek their own, not the things that are Christ's (Phil. 2:21). The Lord comes to dismantle ceiled houses so that His might be finished! He devastates the personal plans of men, turning every structure upside down until His House is set in order (2 Kings 20:1). His fan is in His hand. He will thoroughly purge His floor.

Lk. 15:8, KJV

Either what woman having ten pieces of silver, if she lose one piece, doth not light a candle, and sweep the house, and seek diligently till she find it?

Tabernacles is the feast of ingathering and harvest. Most church growth in America comes from spiritual nomadism. In pursuing revelation knowledge, men sometimes lose their love for lost souls. The "woman," the Church (Eph. 5:22-24), has misplaced her "coin"—the power of redemption, the spirit of evangelism. The Lord is coming to sweep us, to rearrange furniture, to remove clutter. He will rip the house apart until this coin is rediscovered (Ps. 146:9)!

Mt. 21:12-13, KJV

> *And Jesus went into the temple of God, and cast out all them that sold and bought in the temple, and overthrew the tables of the moneychangers, and the seats of them that sold doves,*
>
> *And said unto them, It is written, My house shall be called the house of prayer; but ye have made it a den of thieves.*

The Greek word for "overthrow" here is *katastrepho* (English *catastrophe*) and means "to turn upside down; to upset." It is an intensive form of *strepho*, which means "to twist or reverse." The Day of the Lord is a day of reversals (Ps. 126). The word for "tables" refers to that which is "four-legged," indicating the beast nature. The Greek word for "seats" is *kathedra* (English *cathedral*) and it means "a bench." It is derived from *hedraios*, which means "to sit sedentary; immovable."

Jn. 2:15-16, KJV

> *And when He had made a scourge of small cords, He drove them all out of the temple, and the sheep, and the oxen; and poured out the changers' money, and overthrew the tables;*

> *And said unto them that sold doves, Take these things hence; make not My Father's house an house of merchandise.*

Thank God for a scourge of "small" cords; the Greek diminutive shows that in wrath He remembers mercy (Hab. 3:2). The word for "scourge" is *phragellion* and means "a whip; a Roman lash as a public punishment." The Day of the Lord will reveal all things openly.

Jesus overthrew the tables of the moneychangers in the beginning (Jn. 2) and ending (Mt. 21) of His public ministry. Jehovah's house of "prayer" had become a house of "merchandise," the Greek word *emporion* (English *emporium*). *Vine's* adds, "a place of trading or exchange." Its verb form means "to travel for business; to traffic, trade; to make a gain, to make merchandise of." This also vividly portrays "Christian" professionals who traffic their wares from city to city, merchandising the gospel in sermon and song, selling doves. The "Christian" emporium is big business. There, for the love of money and fame, men feverishly franchise their giftings and callings for a mess of pottage (Gen. 25:29-34).

Men have "exchanged" the image of the incorruptible for the corruptible (Rom. 1:23-25). Christ is the image of God; antichrist is any other image (2 Cor. 4:4). As noted, the "mark" of the beast is a present reality; idols are "graven" (the same word) by art and man's device, the wisdom and strength of the flesh (Acts 17:29). Things that impress mere men are foolishness to God. Jesus defined a "thief" as one who climbs in by some other way (Jn. 10:1). The house of prayer has become a den of thieves, a heart that wants covenant with God on its own terms. The spirit of antichrist (which means "instead of Christ") pursues everything except the anointing.

At the beginning of this age, Jesus cleansed His Church and threw out all the crooks and con artists. In these last days, He is about to tip the tables again. Men and women unashamedly prostitute their ministries, contracting for minimum nightly amounts. Bodyguards are expensive. No one is that important. Come, Lord Jesus. You are the Potter; we are the clay (Is. 29:16). Sanctify Your people. Restore, remake us. Overthrow the tables of men and demons. Cleanse Your temple. Build Your house until we are a habitation of prayer and peace!

2 Kings 21:13, NIV

...I will wipe out Jerusalem as one wipes a dish, wiping it and turning it upside down.

I Will Overthrow the Throne of Kingdoms

Hag. 2:22, KJV

And I will overthrow the throne of kingdoms....

Haggai prophesies the first "overthrow." This word means "to turn about or over; by implication, to change, overturn, return, pervert." *Vine's* adds, "to turn back, transform." It is found almost 100 times in biblical Hebrew, mentioned first in Genesis 3:24. This word describes the "overthrow" of Sodom and Gomorrah, the Midianites, and Nineveh (Gen. 19:29; Judg. 7:13; Jon. 3:4). Consider also Job 28:9, Proverbs 12:7, and Amos 8:10.

The word "throne" is singular and is used collectively. The same spirit of antichrist sits in the seat or throne of every counterfeit kingdom (2 Thess. 2:3-4). The beast nature—sinful man—rules in each and every one of them. He is at war with the Lamb whose throne is above every other. The word for "throne" in Haggai 2:22 speaks of that which is "covered; a throne (as canopied)." *Vine's* adds "seat," with the basic meaning "seat of honor." It is translated in the King James Version as "seat, stool, throne." It comes from a primitive root that means "to plump, fill up hollows; by implication, to cover (for clothing or secrecy)," and it is especially mentioned in the Book of Isaiah (Is. 14:9,13; 47:1). By comparison, the Greek word *thronos* means "a stately seat; power, a potentate." The singular *throne* of Haggai 2:22 is the "seat" of satan, the seat of the beast (Rev. 2:13; 13:2; 16:10). In every life and ministry, God must overthrow and remove the throne of the kingdoms, the seat of iniquity—all authority outside of Christ (Ps. 94:20; Jonah 3:6). The apostle Paul explains this *removal* of lesser gods.

2 Cor. 10:4-5, NIV

The weapons we fight with are not the weapons of the world. On the contrary, they have divine power to demolish strongholds.

We demolish arguments and every pretension that sets itself up against the knowledge of God, and we take captive every thought to make it obedient to Christ.

The notorious "mark" in Revelation 13:17 means "a stamp or impression." Man's thoughts are impressions, the mark of the beast. These become the image of the beast, the things men worship, idolize, and follow. The image then becomes the beast itself, the "strong holds" of Second Corinthians 10:4. Ask any preacher who has built his own kingdom...once the monster is created, it must be fed! Don't be afraid, children. Monsters aren't real.

2 Thess. 2:3-4, KJV

> *Let no man deceive you by any means: for that day shall not come, except there come a falling away first, and that man of sin be revealed, the son of perdition;*
>
> *Who opposeth and exalteth himself above all that is called God, or that is worshipped; so that he as God sitteth in the temple of God, shewing himself that he is God.*

The carnal mind enthrones itself in the temple, the *naos* of God (Hag. 1:2). The only thing the serpent eats is dust; to be carnally minded is death (Is. 65:25; Rom. 8:6). The Lord intends to demolish every argument and pretension that exalts itself against His Word. He will overthrow and remove every offense. There are territorial spirits over cities and regions (Eph. 6:12); living and moving in the souls of men, they can have a strong hold on our minds. Everything is to be recaptured by the anointing. Jesus defeated the devil and dismantled his kingdom (Col. 2:15; 1 Jn. 3:8). Appropriate His victory and eternal triumph. Be renewed in the spirit of your mind.

Man's seat of reasoning is depicted by Eli, the priest who would not restrain his sons (1 Sam. 4:18). Heavy of flesh and going blind, this way of thinking is about to collapse and come down. There is an existing Eli; but there is a growing Samuel, a prophetic people who will set the heart of the nation back upon God and the founding vision. Moreover, there are two women in the Book of Proverbs: the strange woman (Prov. 7) and the virtuous woman (Prov. 31). The Book of Revelation identifies them as the harlot (Rev. 17–18) and the Bride (Rev. 19). In New Covenant realities, the realm of spirit is masculine, while the soul realm is feminine. Two women represent two kinds of minds, two attitudes. The estranged mindset is seated in pride (Prov. 9:14). Every usurper will abdicate his throne in the Day of the Lord. Jesus alone is the rightful Ruler of our hearts (Hag. 2:23).

Ezek. 26:16, NIV

> *Then all the princes of the coast will step down from their thrones and lay aside their robes and take off their embroidered garments. Clothed with terror, they will sit on the ground, trembling every moment....*

God will overthrow the throne of "kingdoms." This is the Hebrew word *mamlakah* (Strong's #4467); it means "dominion; the estate (rule), or the country (realm)." *Vine's* adds, "reign or rule; sovereignty, dominion." It comes from a primitive root that means "to reign; inceptively, to ascend the throne; causatively, to induct into royalty; hence (by implication) to take counsel." This word for "kingdom" is peculiar to the Book of Psalms (see Ps. 46:6; 68:32; 102:22; 135:11), the Book of Isaiah (see Is. 10:10; 13:4; 23:11; 47:5), and the Book of Jeremiah (Jer. 1:10; 10:7; 51:20). Its Hebrew root denotes:

1. *The territory of the kingdom (Esther 1:4).*

2. *Anything royal or kingly (Esther 1:7-11).*

3. *The year of rule (Esther 2:16).*

4. *The accession to the throne (Esther 4:14).*

All these meanings are associated with the Greek word *basileia*, the major translation of *mamlakah* in the Septuagint. The New Testament authors used this word to refer to God's "kingdom"—the realm, the king, the sovereignty, and the relationship to God Himself. Throughout the Old Testament, God promised to undo all other kingdoms besides His own:

1. *In Nimrod's day (Gen. 10:10).*

2. *In Moses' day (1 Sam. 10:18).*

3. *In Joshua's day (Deut. 3:21; Josh. 11:10).*

4. *In David's day (1 Chron. 29:30).*

5. *In Solomon's day (1 Kings 4:21).*

6. *In Jehoshaphat's day (2 Chron. 20:6,29).*

7. *In Amos' day (Amos 9:8).*

The message is clear. Every other affection will be shaken and removed in the Day of the Lord (Zeph. 3:8). Then each of us will be a house of prayer, the place of unshakeable peace and unbroken covenant. Jesus will have our whole heart, the whole dominion.

I Will Destroy the Strength of the Kingdoms

Hag. 2:22, KJV

...I will destroy the strength of the kingdoms of the heathen....

The prophet declares the second overthrow. The word for "destroy" in this verse is *shamad* (Strong's #8045) and means "to desolate." *Vine's* adds, "to annihilate, exterminate." It is rendered in the King James Version as "destroy, destruction, bring to nought, overthrow, perish, pluck down." This word is used in Deuteronomy 7:24; 9:3,14 and Joshua 24:8 to describe Israel's commission to possess Canaan. The house of the wicked will be destroyed (Ps. 37:38; 92:7; Prov. 14:11).

God will overthrow the "strength" of heathen kingdoms. This word means "power; to fasten upon, to seize, be strong; figuratively, courageous; to bind, conquer." Any beastly thing or person that has fastened itself upon our lives will be shaken loose (Zech. 4:6; Acts 28:1-5). Our only source of strength will be His joy. The word for "heathen" in verse 22 is the same one that is used in Haggai 2:7,14. Everything alien, within and without, is subdued in the name of the Lord. Hail, King Jesus, the Conqueror of our hearts!

I Will Overthrow the Chariots

Hag. 2:22, KJV

...I will overthrow the chariots, and those that ride in them....

Haggai proclaims the third overthrow. The word for "chariots" means "a seat (in a vehicle)" and it is taken from a primitive root that means "to ride (on an animal or in a vehicle); to place upon (for riding), to despatch." *Vine's* says that this word represents a "war-chariot" (Ex. 14:25), which may have been used as a "chariot of honor"; Genesis 41:43 is its first mention. The chariot rivalled the bow in its effectiveness as a weapon; only wealthier nations could establish and maintain a chariot force. The first chariots mentioned in the Bible belonged to Egypt (Ex. 14:6-9; 15:4). At first, the nation of Israel rejected chariots as tools of warfare (Josh. 11:4-9). Solomon, however, developed a chariot corps in his army (1 Kings 4:26; 9:19; 10:29). The chariot, along with the horse and rider, represents the strength of Egypt (the world), the strength of man, the strength of the flesh (2 Sam. 15:1; 2 Chron. 9:25; Mic. 5:10). But the battle is the Lord's!

Mic. 1:13, KJV

O thou inhabitant of Lachish, bind the chariot to the swift beast: she is the beginning of the sin to the daughter of Zion: for the transgressions of Israel were found in thee.

The word for "ride" in Haggai 2:22 comes from the same root word as "chariot." *Vine's* adds, "to ride upon, drive, mount (an animal)." Every ceiled house comes with a three-car garage—for the world, the flesh, and the devil. These vehicles of compromise and spiritual ease are not allowed on the highway back to Zion. Not geared for steep ascents, they've carried the flesh as far as they can go. From here on, you'll have to get out and walk!

"and the horses and their riders shall come down..." (Hag. 2:22b). The word for "horse" in verse 22 is *cuwc* (Strong's #5483) and means "to skip (properly, for joy); a horse (as leaping); also a swallow (from its rapid flight)."

The first biblical appearance of the "horse" is in Genesis 47:17. It was not until the end of the second millennium B.C. that a rudimentary cavalry appeared on the battlefield. In the period of the eighth-century B.C. prophets and following, horses became a sign of luxury and apostasy (Is. 2:7; Amos 4:10). Inasmuch as Israel's hope for freedom and security was to be the Lord, her kings were commanded not to multiply horses (Deut. 17:15-16). The prophet Jeremiah used the symbol of a well-fed horse to describe the idolatry and unfaithfulness of God's people (Jer. 5:8). The word for "riders" in verse 22 is the same as "ride." They shall be smitten with confusion and madness in the Day of the Lord (Zech. 10:5; 12:4).

Ex. 15:1, KJV

...I will sing unto the Lord, for He hath triumphed gloriously: the horse and his rider hath He thrown into the sea.

The strength of the flesh must "come down." This word in Haggai 2:22 means "to descend (literally, to go downwards; or conventionally to a lower region; figuratively, to fall)." This word is used frequently of dying. One "goes down" to his grave (Is. 38:18-19). This word is also used to indicate "coming away from" the altar (Lev. 9:22), the opposite of *alah* or "ascending to" the altar, going up to the mountain (Hag. 1:8). The varied uses of the former verb show how the personal idols of men will tip over in the day of global cataclysm. The "going down" of a city is its destruction (Deut. 20:20). When a day "descends," it comes to an end (Judg. 19:11).

The "descent" of a shadow is its lengthening (2 Kings 20:11). Tears "flow down" the cheeks when one weeps bitterly (Jer. 13:17). This word is also used figuratively of a "descent in social position" (Deut. 28:43).

"...every one by the sword of his brother" (Hag. 2:22). The words "every one" in verse 22 show all human genius humbled in the Day of the Lord. The phrase comes from the root *anash* which means "a mortal; to be frail, feeble, or melancholy." The latter is translated in the King James Version as "desperate, incurable, sick, woeful," and reveals the innate weakness of mortal wisdom and strength. The word for "sword" in Haggai 2:22 is *chereb* (Strong's #2719), and it means "drought; also a cutting instrument (from its destructive effect), as a knife, sword, or other sharp implement." Its root means "to parch (through drought); (by analogy,) to desolate, destroy, kill." The weapons of our warfare are not carnal. Saul's fleshly armor is useless in the Day when the Church finally understands that the war is over (1 Sam. 17:38-39; Mic. 4:3). Jesus fought and won it at the cross!

Is. 40:2, KJV

Speak ye comfortably to Jerusalem, and cry unto her, that her warfare is accomplished....

The word for "brother" in Haggai 2:22 is used in the widest sense of literal relationship and metaphorical affinity or resemblance. It is translated in the King James Version as "another, brother, brotherly; kindred, like, other." This word can indicate a companion or colleague, a brother by choice, or an ally (Ps. 49:7; Prov. 18:9). Every ungodly relationship, every unholy alliance and confederation will be broken in the day of unshakeable peace (Ps. 2:1-3; Ezek. 38:21). All that will remain are godly relationships that cannot be moved. As in the days of Gideon, Jonathan, and Jehoshaphat, the enemies of righteousness will turn upon themselves (Judg. 7:22; Sam. 14:16; 2 Chron. 20:22). The world will devour itself.

Is. 19:2, KJV

> *And I will set the Egyptians against the Egyptians: and they shall fight every one against his brother, and every one against his neighbour; city against city, and kingdom against kingdom.*

The *prince* of unshakeable peace, Jesus Christ, will be given whole dominion. This entire section (Hag. 2:20-22) conveys and declares the dismissal of every other kingdom. The throne of Babylon is coming down in one day (Is. 47:1; Rev. 18:1-8). This was evidenced in the Samaritan uprising (Ezra 4), a mongrel race of compromisers and idolaters, they exemplify this spirit of antichrist and anarchy, the mixed bag of all secondhand thrones and kingdoms. The voice of God brings this individual shaking, the *removal* of all things that offend out of His Kingdom (Mt. 13:41). The word from the mouth of His prophets separates the precious from the vile (Is. 60:12; Jer. 15:19).

The prophet Daniel visualized the results of this cosmic convulsion. His Kingdom will stand (Dan. 2:35,44; 7:27)! The apostle John, who envisioned the same victorious reign of God, was caught up into the spirit of the

Day of the Lord, the day of ultimate triumph (Rev. 11:15). God will get Himself honor upon Pharaoh and all the chariots of Egypt (Ex. 14:17,28; Ps. 46:9). In that day, His dominion will be from sea to sea (Zech. 9:10). There will be no place to hide, no false hope of imminent evacuation when the Lord punishes the high ones of the earth (Is. 2:19; 24:21). He will destroy everything that comes against His habitation of peace (Zech. 12:9).

After the *removal*, all that stands is the *Ruler* Himself! With all enemies under His feet, Jesus Christ is Lord, the supreme, sovereign God whose name is above all others (Phil. 2:9-11). He will build His Church! To Him be all glory!

Chapter Ten

The Ruler

"...I will make thee as a signet..."

Haggai 2:23

The crowning verse of Haggai's prophecy refocuses upon the crux of his message: The primary characteristic of the latter house of greater glory will be an *unshakeable peace* in the time of global shaking. The Lord has determined to oust the strength of every throne and chariot (Hag. 2:20-22). In verse 23 Jesus Christ is our heavenly Zerubbabel, the Conqueror of every enemy, the only One with power to topple the kingdoms of our hearts. He has been given all executive authority in heaven and earth. True worshipers who give Him their whole heart (Hag. 2:10-19) will concede to Him the whole dominion (Hag. 2:20-23).

Note and compare the three uses of "saith the Lord" in Haggai 2:23 with the triple overthrowing in verse 22. The phrase "saith the Lord" or "saith the Lord of hosts" is used frequently throughout Haggai's prophecy. The word "saith" comes from a root that means "to whisper, to utter as an oracle." The word of His lordship is heard with the inner ear of the hidden man of the heart, and can only be discerned through pure worship (1 Kings 19:12).

Hag. 2:23, KJV

In that day, saith the Lord of hosts, will I take thee, O Zerubbabel, My servant, the son of Shealtiel, saith the Lord, and will make thee as a signet: for I have chosen thee, saith the Lord of hosts.

Hag. 2:23, NIV

"On that day...I will make you like My signet ring, for I have chosen you," declares the Lord Almighty.

Hag. 2:23, TLB

...and honor you like a signet ring upon My finger; for I have specially chosen you....

Hag. 2:23, Knox

...on that day I will take thee to My side, keep thee there, close as signet-ring....

Hag. 2:23, AMP

...for I have chosen you [as the one with whom to renew My covenant to David's line]....

Haggai concludes his literary ministry with a personal word to Zerubbabel, revoking the sentence pronounced upon his grandfather Jehoiachin (Jer. 22:24). Ultimately, this word prognosticates the Messiah and

His family (Rev. 3:21). The Greek word for "throne" is *thronos* and means "the place or seat of authority." Jesus' "throne" is singular, contrasting all other thrones; His is the name above every other. He is the Chief Apostle, the highest authority in the Church (Heb. 3:1). Contrast this with the "throne," the seat of the beast mentioned in Haggai 2:22.

The exegesis of Haggai's magnificent prophecy has unfolded the deep things of God. Yet his simple message is that God will complete His purposed will in each of our lives! This absolute truth is most vividly portrayed by Haggai's prophetic peer, then confirmed in both Testaments.

Zech. 4:9, KJV

The hands of Zerubbabel have laid the foundation of this house; his hands shall also finish it; and thou shalt know that the Lord of hosts hath sent me unto you.

Zech. 4:9, NIV

...his hands will also complete it....

Ps. 138:8, KJV

The Lord will perfect that which concerneth me....

Ps. 138:8, NIV

The Lord will fulfill His purpose for me....

Jer. 29:11, KJV

For I know the thoughts that I think toward you, saith the Lord, thoughts of peace, and not of evil, to give you an expected end.

Jer. 29:11, NIV

...to give you hope and a future.

Phil. 1:6, KJV

Being confident of this very thing, that He which hath begun a good work in you will perform it until the day of Jesus Christ.

Phil. 1:6, NIV

...will carry it on to completion....

The Person and finished work of our Lord Jesus Christ, the heavenly governor of Judah, is the *surety*, *guarantee*, and *assurance* of the New Covenant. The new creation reality of the finished temple is the formation of Christ within an overcoming people (Gal. 4:19).

The "signet ring" vision is to be fulfilled in "that day," a familiar phrase to the prophets. "That day" in the Old Covenant is "this day" in the New Covenant. The broad sense of "this day" is the New Testament day. The present application of "this day" is the third day, the Day of the Lord, the day when He comes to be admired and glorified in His holy habitation (2 Thess. 1:10). The use of "that day" is most prominent among the prophets, especially the Book of Isaiah (see Is. 4:1-2; 10:27; 11:10; 22:20; 52:6) and the Book of Zechariah (Zech. 12:3-11; 13:1-4; 14:4-13). Compare Amos 9:11, Micah 4:6, and Malachi 3:17.

"Take Thee...Make Thee"

The special word to the governor of Judah is, "I will take thee...and will make thee..." (Hag. 2:23). This truth

is illustrated by Jesus in the "lost and found" chapter—
Luke 15—a lost sheep, a lost coin, a lost son. The latter is
the story of two prodigals, one who strayed and one who
stayed (Lk. 15:11-20). The initial cry of the younger son
was "give me"! Content to leave home with but part of
his inheritance, he wasted his substance with riotous
living. When he repented and returned to his father's
house, his cry was "make me...."

Zerubbabel is to be taken or apprehended as the
chosen of God. The verb for "take" means "to take,
grasp, take hold of." A secondary meaning is "to take to
oneself." All things were created by and for Him (Col.
1:16). This word carries the idea of special selection (Ex.
6:7; Josh. 24:3; 2 Sam. 7:8). We have been apprehended
(Phil. 3:12-14). In the absolute sense of the word, God
"took away" Enoch (Gen. 5:24; Ps. 49:15; 73:24). The
word for "make" here in Haggai 2:23 is part of the word
for "consider" in Haggai 1:5, and it means "to put, place,
set, or fix." In its first biblical appearance, it means "to
put or place someone somewhere" (Gen. 2:8). Another
positive use of the word means "to appoint" (1 Sam. 8:5),
or "to put clothing on, setting it down upon one's body"
(Ruth 3:3). "To place or put something on one's heart"
means to consider (Is. 47:7) or pay heed to it (1 Sam.
21:12). This word also means "to fix something in a particular place" or "to continue or preserve" (Gen. 24:47;
45:7). Governor Zerubbabel prefigures the Messiah.

All these applications of the word for "make" refer to
the last Adam, the federal Head of the new creation. Our
King is the set Man in Zion, the Word forever settled in
Heaven (Ps. 2:6; 119:89). Jacob was created, but Israel, the

new creation man, was formed (Is. 43:1). Only God can make us to become like Jesus (Ps. 100:3; Phil. 2:13).

My Servant

Zerubbabel is then called "My servant" by the Lord (Hag. 2:22). This Hebrew word comes from a root that means "to work, serve, till; to be enslaved." Compare this with the Greek word *doulos*, or "bondslave." Isaiah declared the Messiah to be the Servant of Jehovah (see Is. 42:1-7; 49:1-7; 50:4-10; 52:13-53:12). The governor of Judah is thus likened to Moses, the servant of the Lord (Num. 12:7; Josh. 1:1-2). Zerubbabel would follow in the steps of his ancestor David, the man after God's heart (Ezek. 34:23; 37:24).

When the apostle admonished us to have the mind of Christ (Phil. 2:4-5), the heart attitude of genuine humility, he recaptured the essence of Haggai's prophecy. Every man was running to his own private life while the house of God lay waste. Those who wear Zerubbabel's signet ring look to the interests of the Lord and His purposes in the earth. True Israelites who have power with God and men are servants of all (Is. 43:10; Mk. 10:44-45). Our apostolic boast? We are part of the privileged class—the slaves of Jesus (Rom. 1:1).

I Will Make Thee as a Signet

Zerubbabel was a seal guaranteeing the fulfillment of God's promise given to David (2 Sam. 7:12-16). He was chosen, not by the people or even mighty Cyrus. This petty prince from Judah (Ezra 1:8), a small impoverished nation under foreign dominance, was honored by the supreme Ruler, the Lord of hosts. Sheshbazzar, born and

so named in Babylon, was a prominent link in the il-
lustrious Messianic chain extending from King David to
King Jesus (Mt. 1:1, 12-13). The prophet declares the post-
exilic Governor of Judah to be a "signet." This word is
chowtham (Strong's #2368) and means "a signature-ring."
It is translated in the King James Version as "seal, signet," and is taken from a primitive root that means "to
close up; especially, to seal." The latter is rendered as
"make an end, seal (up), stop" in the King James Version.

The signet was a precious stone on which was
engraved the name, some identifying emblem, or design
of the owner. A medallion or ring featured a raised or
recessed signature or symbol that could be impressed on
wax on moist clay. The signet was stamped into soft clay
tablets (on which business, legal, or other important mat-
ters were inscribed), and allowed to harden (Job 38:14).
If papyrus or parchment was used, the seal was im-
printed on wax or clay discs affixed to the documents,
then declared authentic. The seal or ring was an official's
personal signature. Pharoah gave his signet to Joseph
as a badge of delegated authority (Gen. 41:42). Ahasuerus gave his ring to the wicked Haman, then to Mor-
decai after Haman's treachery was exposed (Esther
3:10-12; 8:2). King Darius of Persia sealed Daniel in the
lion's den (Dan. 6:17). Highly cherished and carefully
guarded against any possible loss, the seal was worn
constantly on the king's person—on his finger (Jer.22:4);
carried on a cord around his neck (see the "bracelet" of
Gen. 38:18), hence, near the heart (Song 8:6); or fastened
to his arm. Compare First Kings 21:8; Nehemiah 9:38;
10:1; and Jeremiah 32:10-14,44. The signet was an emblem
of royal authority, a most prized possession, the power

of attorney—the *name* of the owner. Zerubbabel, who had been designated by God to lead the returning captives back to Jerusalem, was thus invested with the highest honor.

All these thoughts about the signature-ring reveal the preciousness and power of Jesus' *name*. Every ring requires a finger. Jesus compared "the finger of God" (Lk. 11:20) with "the Spirit of God" (Mt. 12:28). True Kingdom authority must be by the power and nature of the Holy Spirit, the Spirit of the Son (Gal. 4:6-7).

Rom. 14:17, KJV

> *For the kingdom of God is...in the Holy Ghost.*

The Chosen of the Lord

Zerubbabel typifies the Messiah and his glorious Church as the "chosen" or elect of God (Mt. 12:18; 1 Pet. 2:4), the house where God has foreordained to pour out the glory of unshakeable peace. This word in Haggai 2:23 means "to try, to select," and is translated in the King James Version as "acceptable, appoint, choose, excellent, require." This verb is found 170 times throughout the Old Testament. In more than half of the occurrences, God is the subject.

Neh. 9:7-8, NIV

> *You are the Lord God, who chose Abram and brought him out of Ur of the Chaldeans and named him Abraham.*
>
> *You found his heart faithful to You, and You made a covenant with him....*

Being chosen by God brings people into an intimate relationship with Him (Deut. 14:1-2). God's choices shaped the history of Israel, led to their redemption from Egypt (Deut. 7:6-8), sent Moses and Aaron to work miracles there (Ps. 105:26-27), and gave them the Levites to bless in the name of the Lord (Deut. 21:5). He chose their inheritance, including Jerusalem, where He dwelt among them (see Deut. 12:5; 2 Chron. 6:5,21; Ps. 47:4). The Septuagint translates this word chiefly by *eklegein*. The verb is used of God's or Christ's choice of men for service or as the objects of His grace (Lk. 6:13; Eph. 1:4). John's gospel sums up this central truth of divine election.

Jn. 15:16, KJV

Ye have not chosen Me, but I have chosen you, and ordained you, that ye should go and bring forth fruit, and that your fruit should remain: that whatsoever ye shall ask of the Father in My name, He may give it you.

A careful study of Zerubbabel being Jehovah's "chosen" will reveal much about the Messiah and the Church who shares His authority. This word is used with particular emphasis throughout the Book of Psalms (see Ps. 25:12; 65:4; 84:10; 105:26; 132:13) and the Book of Proverbs (see Prov. 1:29; 3:31; 8:10; 10:20; 16:16; 21:2). Compare Joshua 24:15, First Chronicles 15:2; and Zechariah 1:17.

The Authority of King Jesus

Mt. 28:18, NIV

Then Jesus came to them and said, "All authority in heaven and on earth has been given to Me."

All truths concerning the "seal" originate in the Pattern Son. Jesus Christ could not be sealed by the strongest governments of this world. Our heavenly Zerubbabel was stamped with the Father's approval (Mt. 27:66; Jn. 6:27). Jesus has the signet. Jesus *is* the signet! Both testaments set forth His sovereign authority over all things. He alone wears the signature-ring, having been given jurisdiction over heaven and earth. The Old Testament attests to His government (Mic. 5:2), especially in the Book of Psalms (see Ps.2:6; 8:5-8; 45:6-7; 72:17-19; 91:14; 110:1-3) and in the Book of Isaiah (see Is. 22:24; 40:10; 52:7,13; 55:4).

Dan. 7:14, KJV

And there was given Him dominion, and glory, and a kingdom, that all people, nations, and languages, should serve Him: His dominion is an everlasting dominion, which shall not pass away, and His kingdom that which shall not be destroyed.

Though predicted in the Old Testament, one must turn to the New Covenant to fully appreciate the absolute authority of the One whom the Father has sealed:

1. *The Synoptic Gospels (see Mt. 2:6; 7:29; 10:1; 11:27; 16:19, 28; Lk. 1:32-33; 5:24; 10:22).*

2. *The Gospel of John (see Jn. 3:31, 35-36; 5:22; 13:3; 15:16; 16:15; 17:1-3)*

3. *The Book of Acts (see Acts 2:32-36; 3:13; 5:31; 10:36).*

4. *The Pauline epistles (see Rom. 14:9-11; 1 Cor. 11:3; 15:24-27; Eph. 1:20-23; Phil. 2:9-11; 3:21).*

5. *The general epistles (see Heb. 1:1-4; 2:8-9; 12:2; 1 Pet. 1:21; 3:22; 2 Pet. 1:3,16-17).*

6. *The Book of Revelation (see Rev. 1:5; 3:21; 5:12; 6:2; 10:1-2; 11:15; 12:10; 17:14; 19:12,16).*

The One who has all might and power has purposed to share it with His eternal companion of like nature and ability, the Bride of Christ! We have been predestined to be joint-heirs of His grace and life (Rom. 8:17,28-31; 1 Pet. 3:7). By Him kings reign and princes decree justice (Prov. 8:15).

Col. 1:16-17, NIV

For by Him all things were created: things in heaven and on earth, visible and invisible, whether thrones or powers or rulers or authorities; all things were created by Him and for Him.

He is before all things, and in Him all things hold together.

The Triple Sealing

The revelatory understanding of the triple sealing was imparted to my life almost 25 years ago through the anointed writings of Bill Britton, a great literary prophet from Springfield, Missouri. That message is still in print (call 417-865-1075 for further information). Jehovah inscribed Zion on the palms of His hands (Is. 49:16). In the New Covenant, the New Jerusalem is the Church, the city of the living God (Mt. 5:14; Heb. 12:22-24).

2 Tim. 2:19, TLB

But God's truth stands firm like a great rock, and nothing can shake it. It is a foundation stone with these words written on it: "The Lord knows those who are really His...."

The Greek word for "seal" is *sphragis* (Strong's #4973), and it means "a signet (a fencing in or protecting from misappropriation); the stamp impressed (as a mark of privacy or genuineness." It is derived from *phrasso* (Strong's #5420), which means "to fence or enclose; to block up, to silence." Its root is *phren* (Strong's #5424), the word for "the midrif; figuratively, the feelings; by extension, the mind or cognitive faculties." The latter is translated in the King James Version as "understanding." *Vine's* Dictionary adds that *sphragis* is an emblem expressing ownership, authentication, permanency, and security with a view to destination, the persons "sealed" are secured from destruction and marked for reward!

The *purpose* of unshakeable peace is to complete the real temple, to save the whole man—spirit, soul, and body. Jesus Christ is set forth in the Book of Hebrews as our great High Priest, the heavenly Jeshua. A careful study of the sacred garments of Aaron reveals *three* sets of seals on his robes and headpiece (Ex. 28:11,21,36). The High Priest in full three-layered dress gloriously portrays the new creation Man standing in the magnificent majesty of total redemption. This triple sealing powerfully restates the spiritual law of "excellent" or threefold things (Prov. 22:20). That rule of biblical hermeneutics is briefly summarized in the exegesis of Haggai 1:1-2; 2:15,22. As noted, the three dimensions of Moses' Tabernacle and the three major Feasts of the Lord are foundational to this principle. Another basic parallel is Aaron's high priestly vesture; marked for glory and beauty (Ex. 28:2), he was graced with three signets. This chart of the signets overviews and unfolds their splendid prediction, and captures the essence of unshakeable peace.

First Signet	Second Signet	Third Signet
Ex. 28:21; 39:14	Ex. 28:11; 39:6	Ex. 28:36; 39:30
Breastplate	Onyx stones	Gold plate
Heart	Hand (arm)	Head
First sealing	Second sealing	Third sealing
Rom. 4:11	Eph. 1:13; 4:30	Rev. 7:3; 14:1; 22:4
Water baptism	Spirit baptism	Mind of Christ
Peace that loves	Peace that lifts	Peace that laughs
Peace that gives	Peace that guards	Peace that governs

The First Signet

Ex. 28:21, KJV

And the stones shall be with the names of the children of Israel, twelve, according to their names, like the engravings of a signet; every one with his name shall they be according to the twelve tribes.

The first "signet" or seal was the breastplate that covered the heart of the High Priest (Ex. 28:15-30). Like the veil, it was made with gold, blue, purple, scarlet, and fine twined linen, all representing the divine nature of Jesus Christ. Each of the twelve stones, inscribed with the names of the tribes of Israel, is a specific aspect of that new nature (2 Cor. 5:17).

Song 8:6, KJV

Set me as a seal upon thine heart....

Mt. 15:19, NIV

For out of the heart come evil thoughts, murder, adultery, sexual immorality, theft, false testimony, slander.

The breastplate covered the heart! When the heart is sealed, the works of the flesh are cut off (Gal. 5:19-21). Aaron's first signet pictures the experience of the new birth and the sealing of that conversion with water baptism in the name of the Lord. The apostle Paul explained in Romans 2:28-29 and Colossians 2:11-12 that Abraham and his seed must experience circumcision, a sign of the cutting away of the flesh. The New Covenant requires a spiritual circumcision of the heart.

He that believes and is baptized shall be saved (Mk. 16:16). In the Feast of Passover, we name Jesus Christ as our personal Savior. The old nature is cut off by the operation of the Spirit. We put on his breastplate and become partakers of the divine nature (2 Pet. 1:3). We receive peace with God—peace that loves, peace that gives.

The Second Signet

Ex. 28:11, KJV

With the work of an engraver in stone, like the engravings of a signet, shalt thou engrave the two stones with the names of the children of Israel: thou shalt make them to be set in ouches of gold.

The second "signet" or seal was comprised of the two onyx stones mounted in gold settings on the shoulders of the High Priest, upon them were also engraved the names of the twelve tribes (Ex. 28:6-14). Two is the number of witness, and it is very significant in connection with the Feast of Pentecost (Lev. 23:17; Acts 1:8; 5:32).

The first sealing deals with the heart and the cutting away of fleshly works. The second focuses on power and promise, and it was put on the shoulders. The shoulders, arms, and hands all speak of strength, power, and the ability to rule or govern (Is. 9:6). The second sealing is the Pentecostal experience of the Holy Ghost baptism with the initial evidence of speaking with other tongues (Acts 2:1-4). Paul declared in Romans 8:23, Second Corinthians 1:21, and Ephesians 1:13-14; 4:30 that the Pentecostal blessing is the firstfruits (not the fullness) of the Spirit, the earnest of our inheritance.

A Christian is initially sealed when he is converted and baptized in water. The second sealing comes after that. Pentecost is in part. It is the foretaste, the pledge of the full inheritance (which the early Church did not receive), ready to be revealed in the last time (1 Pet. 1:4-5). This is illustrated when Jeremiah bought the field and sealed the subscribed evidence (Jer. 32:10-14). He knew that one day God would turn the captivity of Judah, that they would return to the land of their inheritance. Haggai helped fulfill that glorious promise. Like many today, some did not believe God's prophet. Those who lived in defeat did not buy land or seal deeds. For them, the day of revival and restoration was over. But the Church is coming out of Babylon! In the midst of our captivity, God gave a seal, a promise that we will return and see the temple finished. Every time a child of God receives the mighty infilling of the Holy Spirit, we see and hear the manifestation of the guarantee that the Lord will fill the latter house of greater glory with unshakeable peace that lifts and guards!

The Third Signet

Ex. 28:36, KJV

And thou shalt make a plate of pure gold, and grave upon it, like the engravings of a signet, HOLINESS TO THE LORD.

The third and final "signet" or seal was the gold plate on the forehead of the High Priest. In Moses' tabernacle, there are not two dimensions, but three; the third room is the Most Holy Place. We have experienced two feasts, Passover and Pentecost. There is one more: the Feast of Tabernacles in the seventh month, the season when God will perfect the Church. The final sealing is the experience of the full mind of Christ. The seal of Jesus' apostleship are overcomers who are completely conformed to His image and likeness (Rom. 15:28; 1 Cor. 9:2; Heb. 3:1). The apostle John saw this finished work in the Book of Revelation (see Rev. 3:21; 7:3; 14:1; 22:4), using the word "seal" over 30 times.

Why is this final sealing in the forehead? As noted, the Greek root word for "seal" means "the mind or cognitive faculties." Our complete sonship has to do with the transformation of the soul, the renewing of the mind. The Church is being transfigured and changed from glory to glory until we receive the full mind of Christ

(Rom. 12:1-2; 2 Cor. 3:18). This experience was set forth in Haggai 2:20-22 as the complete overthrowing and consequent removal of the throne and strength of all other kingdoms (2 Cor. 10:3-6; Rev. 11:15). The finished temple of the New Covenant, sealed "in" the forehead, will have given the Lord Jesus their whole heart and mind, the whole dominion (1 Pet. 1:13).

"Holiness to the Lord" was the engraving on Aaron's headpiece or crown. This is the condition of the fully sealed mind, the *shalom* or wholeness of the the finished house of perfected peace. This is the victor's wreath, a triple sealing, a threefold cord fastened in the heart, the hand, and the head. Three sealings, three experiences, three realities. Three dimensions of unshakeable peace: peace that loves, lifts, and laughs; peace that gives, guards, and governs.

The glorious Church, the latter house of greater anointing, will go forth with the mind of Christ, the power of the Spirit. True compassion will flow out of a new heart. The whole world will behold their witness and set to their seal that God is true (Jn. 3:33). The maturity of that people will be seen and demonstrated by an *unshakeable peace* in the time of global shaking!

Is. 26:3, KJV

Thou wilt keep him in perfect peace, whose mind is stayed on Thee: because he trusteth in Thee.

Phil. 4:7, KJV

And the peace of God, which passeth all understanding, shall keep your hearts and minds through Christ Jesus.

Wisdom is the principal thing, and with all your getting, *get understanding* (Prov. 4:7). Prayerfully read the Epilogue, an overview of Haggai's entire prophecy. Let the Father set His seal upon your heart, your hand, your head. Then, as one of His lively stones, take your place among the resurrected army of peacemakers in His latter house of greater glory.

Chapter Eleven

Epilogue

Hag. 2:23, NIV

"On that day," declares the Lord Almighty, "I will take you, My servant Zerubbabel son of Shealtiel," *declares the Lord, "and I will make you like My signet ring, for I have chosen you," declares the Lord Almighty.*

Gen. 49:10, KJV

The sceptre shall not depart from Judah, nor a law-giver from between his feet, until Shiloh come; and unto him shall the gathering of the people be.

In the face of all opposition, in the midst of catastrophic political changes, the Kingdom promised to David and the scepter assured to Judah would continue till Shiloh came. The Messiah is the Prince of Peace, the greater Son of David, whose Kingdom is an everlasting Kingdom. With the reassurance of this blessed promise, Haggai closes his book.

Hag. 2:9, KJV

> *The glory of this latter house shall be greater than of the former, saith the Lord of hosts: and in this place will I give peace, saith the Lord of hosts.*

The primary characteristic of the latter house of greater glory will be an *unshakeable peace* in the time of global shaking. Unshakeable peace and unbreakable relationships are a product of unbroken covenant, an undivided heart. This revelatory understanding of the end-time was given to the prophet Haggai over 2,500 years ago. As a messenger of the Lord in His message, a window in the Spirit was opened enough for Haggai to peer straight into the realm of eternal Spirit. In this vision Haggai was able to see the day and time when God would create a people for His name and pleasure—a glorious Church who would show forth the stability and permanency of the Lord's unwavering Kingdom.

Ps. 119:165, NIV

> *Great peace have they who love Your law, and nothing can make them stumble.*

What We Must Remember

Phil. 3:1, NIV

> *Finally, My brothers, rejoice in the Lord! It is no trouble for me to write the same things to you again, and it is a safeguard for you.*

Having exegeted this outstanding vision, let us review the major principles and truths of the Book of Haggai that we have studied here.

Chapter One of this book is an introduction, examining Haggai the man, his moment, and message. Haggai was the first post-exilic voice of the Lord raised up to encourage Zerubbabel and the Jewish remnant to finish the rebuilding of the second temple.

Chapters Two, Three, and Four cover the first of Haggai's predictions, and divulge the *purpose* of unshakeable peace—the whole man (Hag. 1:1-15). Our redemption in Christ will save us to the uttermost—spirit, soul, and body. The finishing of Zerubbabel's temple points to the complete formation of His divine nature within the Church, the Body of Christ, the Father's permanent abode of living stones, eternal in the heavens.

Chapter Two begins with the prophet's *rebuke* (Hag. 1:1-4). The remnant had forsaken the house of the Lord for their own private lives. The Church must be delivered from this individual mindset and reconnect to the original corporate vision. God's purposes are familial, consummating in a people—the holy nation, the resurrected army, the many-membered house of the Lord.

Chapter Three brings the *remedy* to this problem (Hag. 1:5-11). Go up to the mountain and bring wood. As living sacrifices, we must ascend the hill of the Lord, the mountain of transformation, and exchange our life for His—the life of sacrifice, obedience, prayer, compliance, and authority. The body of sin becomes the temple of the Holy Ghost, built with the same substance of His life and nature.

Chapter Four tells of the remnant's *resolve* to hear and obey the Word of the Lord (Hag. 1:12-15). Haggai was the Lord's messenger in the Lord's message. Zerubbabel,

Joshua, and the remnant determined in their spirits to resume Jehovah's primary purpose: build the house! We are called to be sovereigns, saviors, and survivors, equipped with His authority, awareness, and ability.

Chapters Five and Six narrate the second of Haggai's prophecies and set forth the scope, the *parameter* of unshakeable peace—the whole earth (Hag. 2:1-9). God has determined to impact every area of our lives.

Chapter Five rehearses the goodness of God. He provides a *remembrance* for His people, taking them back to the time when the temple saw its first glory (Hag. 2:1-5). He would be with them as in the days of Passover and their supernatural deliverance from Egypt. God had not changed. They were not to fear; His strength would finish the good work He had begun.

Chapter Six predicts the coming of Messiah and His brethren. God will shake the heavens and the earth, both the spiritual and natural realms (Hag. 2:6-9). Bones and stones will be moved by His Word. This global seizure will shake loose and *release* the silver and gold in two dimensions: literally, from the nations and denominations; and spiritually, from the imaginations. The spiritual earthquake will release the silver—the redemption of God in a world-wide harvest of souls. It will shake loose the gold—the fruit of the Spirit, the divine nature, within His people. Then the Desire of all nations, they shall come. This end-time Church, the house of the Lord, will be filled with His glory and unshakeable peace! Our covenant with God and men rests in unbreakable relationships and unbroken covenant.

Chapters Seven and Eight discuss the third utterance of the prophet, explaining the *purity* of unshakeable peace—the whole heart given to God in pure worship (Hag. 2:10-19). The latter house of greater glory is a holy nation of sanctified priests with an undivided affection for God.

Chapter Seven manifests our need to *repair* the personal altar, our private devotion to the Lord (Hag. 2:10-14). Holiness is not contagious, but sin is. We want more than just a touch from the Lord and His ministers; we desire to be bone of His bone and flesh of His flesh, to be one with Him in union and communion, His eternal companion of like nature and ability.

Chapter Eight speaks of the immediate *reward* for obedient sons (Hag. 2:15-19). From the day that we resume work on His house—the original vision—He will bless us.

Chapters Nine and Ten conclude with Haggai's fourth and final prediction, a personal word to Zerubbabel, the ancient governor of Judah. He prefigures the *Prince* of unshakeable peace, the Lord with full dominion (Hag. 2:20-23). Jesus Christ has been given all executive authority in Heaven and in earth.

Chapter Nine reiterates the shaking of Heaven and earth, telling of the personal *removal* of the throne and strength of heathen kingdoms (Hag. 2:20-22). The chariots, with their horses and riders, represent the wisdom and strength of men. All will be swallowed up in the Day of the Lord.

Chapter Ten is the last verse of Haggai's prophecy, and points to the *ruler* Himself, the Messiah, the Prince of Peace (Hag. 2:23). Zerubbabel typifies the Lord Jesus Christ, the One who *is* the personification of God's power, the Word made flesh. Jesus' Person and finished work—His death, burial, resurrection, and ascension—is the surety, guarantee, and assurance that God will bring His purposes and our destiny to completion and conclusion. He will seal His new creation three times—in the heart, hand, and head—and build Himself a house, the place of unshakeable peace!

Eph. 2:14, NIV

For He Himself is our peace....

Haggai's Messianic oracle is an unforgettable exposition of the Lord Jesus Christ—His purpose; His parameter and scope of influence; and His purity in and through His glorious Church. Jesus alone is the Prince and King of peace, the Alpha and the Omega, the Beginning and the Ending (Jer. 29:11). God is more confident about His ability to bring His will and purpose to full conclusion in our lives than we are about our ability to fail (Ps. 138:8; Phil. 1:6).

What We Must Do

Prov. 16:3, KJV

Commit thy works unto the Lord, and thy thoughts shall be established.

Is. 26:3, KJV

Thou wilt keep him in perfect peace, whose mind is stayed on Thee....

In the time of global shaking and the distress of nations, God's people need not wring their hands, sweating and fretting. What are we to do? The clear answer from God's infallible Word speaks for itself.

1 Cor. 15:58, NIV

Therefore, my dear brothers, stand firm. Let nothing move you. Always give yourselves fully to the work of the Lord, because you know that your labor in the Lord is not in vain.

Phil. 3:13-14, KJV

...but this one thing I do, forgetting those things which are behind, and reaching forth unto those things which are before,

I press toward the mark for the prize of the high calling of God in Christ Jesus.

Col. 3:1-2, KJV

...seek those things which are above, where Christ sitteth on the right hand of God.

Set your affection on things above, not on things on the earth.

Heb. 12:1, NIV

...let us throw off everything that hinders and the sin that so easily entangles, and let us run with perseverance the race marked out for us.

Let us fix our eyes on Jesus, the author and perfecter of our faith....

The real Feast of Tabernacles is at hand. The greatest days of Church history are about to be written. Ezekiel's army is standing up. Living stones are reconnecting. We have turned back to our first Love.

Ps. 119:165, KJV

> *Great peace have they which love thy law: and nothing shall offend them.*

The Law of God was made flesh and tabernacled among us. Great peace have they who love the Word, and nothing can make them stumble.

There remains a Sabbath-rest for those who love Jesus, the Author and Finisher of *unshakeable peace*!

TAPE CATALOG

To receive a full listing of Pastor Varner's books and tapes, write or call for our current catalog:

Praise Tabernacle
P.O. Box 785
Richlands, NC 28574-0785
(910) 324-5026 or 324-5027

TAPE OF THE MONTH

Each month two cassette tapes are made available by Pastor Varner. These messages are ministered by him and others in the fivefold ministry. You may join this growing list of listeners on a monthly offering basis.

VIDEO CASSETTES

We are just beginning this new avenue of ministry. Presently available are three, two-hour video cassettes on the Book of Ruth. This teaching is a verse-by-verse exegesis concerning the Christian walk from conceptino to perfection, from birth to maturity. Please write or call for more information.

SEMINARS AND CONVENTIONS

There are annual meetings here in Richlands for the Body of Christ. Please inquire for information on the next meeting. There is a team of ministry here at Praise Tabernacle that is available to your local church to teach the principles of restoration and assist in the areas of praise and worship. Please contact Pastor Varner.